RETIREMENT ISSUES, PLANS AND LIFESTYLES

FINANCIAL ASSET MANAGEMENT AND WEALTH IN RETIREMENT

RETIREMENT ISSUES, PLANS AND LIFESTYLES

Additional books in this series can be found on Nova's website at:

https://www.novapublishers.com/catalog/index.php?cPath=23_29&series
p=Retirement+Issues%2C+Plans+and+Lifestyles

Additional e-books in this series can be found on Nova's website at:

https://www.novapublishers.com/catalog/index.php?cPath=23_29&series
pe=Retirement+Issues%2C+Plans+and+Lifestyles

RETIREMENT ISSUES, PLANS AND LIFESTYLES

FINANCIAL ASSET MANAGEMENT AND WEALTH IN RETIREMENT

TERRANCE G. WAVERLY
EDITOR

Nova Science Publishers, Inc.
New York

For permission to use material from this book please contact us:
Telephone 631-231-7269; Fax 631-231-8175
Web Site: http://www.novapublishers.com

Library of Congress Cataloging-in-Publication Data
Library of Congress Cataloging-in-Publication Data
Financial asset management and wealth in retirement / editor, Terrance G. Waverly.
p. cm.
Includes index.
ISBN 978-1-60741-696-8 (hbk.)
1. Cost and standard of living--United States--Econometric models. 2. Retirement income--United States--Econometric models. 3. Retirees--United States--Economic conditions. 4. Wealth--United States--Econometric models.
I. Waverly, Terrance G.
HD6983.F56 2009
332.024'014--dc22
2010016687

Published by Nova Science Publishers, Inc. ✢ New York

CONTENTS

Preface		**vii**
Chapter 1	The Trajectory of Wealth in Retirement *David A. Love, Michael G. Palumbo and Paul A.Smith*	**1**
Chapter 2	Converting Retirement Savings into Income: Annuities and Periodic Withdrawals *Janemarie Mulvey and Patrick Purcell*	**54**
Chapter 3	Will the Demand for Assets Fall When the Baby Boomers Retire? *Congressional Budget Office*	**95**
Index		**125**

PREFACE

This book looks at the 78 million members of the "baby boom" generation who are beginning to retire. After many years of accumulating assets to spend in retirement, they now must decide how to convert these assets into a steady stream of income. Because of the trend away from defined benefit (DB) pensions to defined contribution (DC) plans, such as 401(k)plans, future retirees will be less likely to have a guaranteed stream of income from defined benefit pensions. Furthermore, while Social Security will provide a guaranteed income to most retirees, it will replace only a relatively small portion of their pre-retirement income.

Chapter 1 - As the baby boomers begin to retire, a great deal remains unknown about the evolution of wealth toward the end of life. In this paper, we develop a new measure of household resources that converts total financial, nonfinancial, and annuitized assets into an expected annual amount of wealth per person. We use this measure, which we call "annualized comprehensive wealth," to investigate spend-down behavior among older households in the Health and Retirement Study. Our analysis indicates that, in (real) dollar terms, the median household's wealth declines more slowly than its remaining life expectancy, so that real annualized wealth actually tends to rise with age over retirement. Comparing the estimated age profiles for annualized wealth with profiles simulated from several different life cycle models, we find that a model that takes into account uncertain longevity, uncertain medical expenses, and (for higher-income retirees) intended bequests lines up best with the HRS data.

Chapter 2 - To a worker contemplating retirement, there is perhaps no more important question than "How long will my money last?" Congress has a strong interest in the income security of older Americans because much of their income is either provided directly from public programs like Social Security, or in the case of pensions and retirement accounts, is subsidized through tax deductions and deferrals.

Many retirees must decide how to convert retirement account balances into income and how to preserve the accounts in the face of several kinds of risk.

Chapter 3 - Between 1946 and 1964, some 78 million babies were born in the United States, forming a cohort that has come to be known as the baby-boom generation. When the oldest people in the group turned 62 in 2008, the generation's first members reached the age of eligibility to collect retirement benefits under Social Security and, presumably, began to retire from the workforce. Some economists warn that if the baby- boom generation begins to sell off assets to finance retirement, there could be a steep decline in the demand for assets, particularly stocks (Brooks 2000; Shoven and Schieber 1997; Siegel 1998, Yoo 1994).

The amount of saving by the baby boomers during their working years might already have affected asset markets. Some economists conclude that the increase in baby boomers' demand for assets during their high-saving years explains some of the strength of the stock market over the past two decades (Geanakoplos, Magill, and Quinzii 2004; Lim and Weil 2003). That demand for assets also could have contributed to the increase in the real (inflation-adjusted) price of housing in the 1970s and 1 980s (Mankiw and Weil 1989), although the sharp rise and fall in house prices during the past decade does not appear to be closely linked to demographic factors.

In: Financial Asset Management and Wealth... ISBN: 978-1-60741-696-8
Editor: Terrance G. Waverly

Chapter 1

THE TRAJECTORY OF WEALTH IN RETIREMENT*

*David A. Love, Michael G. Palumbo and Paul A.Smith**

ABSTRACT

As the baby boomers begin to retire, a great deal remains unknown about the evolution of wealth toward the end of life. In this paper, we develop a new measure of household resources that converts total financial, nonfinancial, and annuitized assets into an expected annual amount of wealth per person. We use this measure, which we call "annualized comprehensive wealth," to investigate spend-down behavior among older households in the Health and Retirement Study. Our analysis indicates that, in (real) dollar terms, the median household's wealth declines more slowly than its remaining life expectancy, so that real annualized wealth actually tends to rise with age over retirement. Comparing the estimated age profiles for annualized wealth with profiles simulated from several different life cycle models, we find that a model that takes into account uncertain longevity, uncertain medical expenses, and (for higher-income retirees) intended bequests lines up best with the HRS data.

* This is an edited, reformatted and augmented version of a Federal Reserve Board publication dated January 2008.

Keywords: Retirement wealth; mortality risk; precautionary saving; bequests; risk and uncertainty.

1. Introduction

The adequacy of a household's wealth depends not only on the amount of total resources at the onset of retirement, but also, crucially, on how those resources are spent toward the end of the life cycle. To investigate spend-down patterns, we construct a new measure of the total resources available *per expected year of life* for retired households in the Health and Retirement Study (HRS), which we call "annualized comprehensive wealth." It is a comprehensive measure because in addition to net worth as it is usually defined—the sum of financial and nonfinancial wealth—it also includes the value of Social Security benefits, defined-benefit pension benefits, and, for eligible recipients, transfer payments such as Food Stamps and Supplemental Security Income. Our measure is an *annualized* concept in the sense that it measures wealth per expected year of remaining life per person. If this measure of total resources were either rising or falling sharply in retirement, we would probably want to know why.

By focusing on the trajectory of annualized comprehensive wealth, we are directly examining whether the total amount of resources available to fund spending in retirement tends to fall more or less quickly than life expectancy shortens. This focus provides a clearer picture of spend-down behavior than would come from looking at how the level of wealth alone changes toward the end of the life cycle. That is, the *rate* at which wealth balances decrease in old age is more relevant for thinking about the consumption possibilities available to older retirees than just whether balances decline at all. Annualized comprehensive wealth is a measurement concept that could help to distinguish between reductions in consumption that might result from retirees having insufficient resources to maintain a prior standard of living (a case in which we would expect both annualized wealth and consumption to be low) and the consequences of other motives, such as precautionary savings or intentional bequests (cases in which we would expect annualized wealth to exceed consumption). Whether annualized wealth rises or falls during retirement therefore provides important information about the underlying causes of spending behavior in retirement.[1]

The simplest life cycle model predicts that wealth balances should decline in tandem with remaining years of life, implying a roughly flat trajectory for annualized wealth. Although there are many reasons why actual behavior might differ from predictions of the simplest life cycle model, we would be inclined to interpret a sharp downward trajectory of annualized wealth as evidence that retirees were spending down their balances "too quickly" or that their initial level of resources were "too low"—particularly if the level of annualized wealth was found to reach a low level early in retirement. Using a balanced panel from 1998 to 2004, however, we find that the median value of annualized comprehensive wealth for households over 70 actually rises, from about $24,900 per person per year to about $28,100 per person per year—a net increase of 13 percent over just six years. That is, we find that at the median of the distribution, comprehensive wealth tends to fall more slowly than life expectancy. Looking at the distribution of outcomes, we estimate that more than one-third of households saw their annualized comprehensive wealth rise by more than 25 percent from 1998 through 2004, while only about one-sixth experienced a decrease of 25 percent or more. This distribution of outcomes is surprisingly similar when we look across different age groups, household compositions, and even household incomes. Indeed, even for the median low-income household in the HRS panel, we find that annualized comprehensive wealth increased slightly over the sample period (although the level of resources remained low). The top quintile of households by income, however, experienced the largest increase in annualized wealth, from $58,200 per person per year in 1998 to $69,500 per person per year in 2004. Looking across the retirement period as a whole (and holding a range of household characteristics constant), we estimate that the median value of annualized comprehensive wealth rose from about $22,000 per person per year at age 62 to about $28,000 at age 85.

Moreover, we find that the annualized values of both financial and nonfinancial assets rose over the sample period. Although some of the increase in nonfinancial wealth in retirement seems to have been accounted for by capital gains that accrued to housing between 1998 and 2004, we show that the net rise in annualized wealth over retirement persists even after controlling for capital gains.

Why might households draw down wealth slowly relative to life expectancy? To examine some likely explanations, we assume that households pursue the standard objective of maximizing expected lifetime utility, and we add to the simplest model some elements from previous studies: uncertain longevity (Yaari, 1965; Davies, 1981; Hubbard, 1987; Hurd, 1989), uncertain medical expenses (Palumbo, 1999; French and Jones, 2004a; Anderson, French, and Lam, 2004), and bequest motives (Kotlikoff and Summers, 1981; Hurd, 1987, 1989; Bernheim, 1991; Laitner and Juster, 1996; Dynan, Skinner, and Zeldes, 2002; De Nardi, 2004; Kopczuk and Lupton, 2007). Our simulations indicate that models incorporating either uncertain medical expenses or bequests can generate upward-sloping profiles of annualized wealth. We obtain the closest fit with the data, however, when we incorporate both of these saving motives into the model, in combination with uncertain lifetimes. In particular, we find that the prospect of large medical expenses induces retirees to build a precautionary buffer early on, while a desire to leave a bequest leads them to maintain "excess savings" toward the end of life.

Our paper contributes to several strands of the literature on household saving and wealth. One strand, focusing on the adequacy of retirement wealth, finds that a substantial fraction of aging households are poorly positioned to finance retirement (see Bernheim, 1992; Munnell and Soto, 2005; Mitchell and Moore, 1998) and that the situation may be even worse for younger age groups (Munnell, Webb, and Delorme, 2006).[2] While we find a significant share of households experiencing a decrease in annualized wealth, our results show that the median retiree seems to be building up annualized resources with age.

A related literature focuses on the optimality of observed household savings by comparing empirical data to accumulation patterns predicted by rich specifications of stochastic life cycle models (see Engen, Gale, and Uccello, 1999, 2005; Scholz, Seshadri, and Khitatrakun, 2006). These papers generally find that observed behavior is in line with the predictions generated by the models. These results are also generally consistent with empirical evidence regarding observed declines in consumption at retirement (Hurd and Rohwedder, 2006). Aguiar and Hurst (2005) find, for example, that home production allows retired households to maintain standards of living while spending less, while Blau (2008) shows that an unexpected health shock could trigger an early retirement and a subsequent decline in consumption.[3] Our approach is distinct from these papers in that we do not attempt to explain optimal wealth levels heading into retirement and we do not directly estimate the path of consumption after retirement. Rather, we condition on the level and composition of wealth at retirement and compare observed patterns of changes in annualized wealth in retirement to predictions from several expanded life cycle models to indirectly infer what factors are consistent with the HRS data.

2. DATA

2.1. Methods

We use longitudinal data from the 1998 through 2004 waves of the Health and Retirement Study (HRS). The HRS is a panel of older households that began in 1992 surveying respondents aged 51 to 61 in that year. The HRS has reinterviewed those households every two years and has added several additional cohorts along the way. In 1998, the HRS merged with a similar survey called Aging and Health Dynamics (AHEAD), which covered households aged 70 and over in 1993. The 1998 wave of the HRS also added two additional cohorts: the War Baby cohort (aged 51 to 56 in 1998) and the Children of the Depression cohort (aged 68 to 74 that year). Thus, the 1998 wave is the first to represent the full population of U.S. households aged 51 and over.

In selecting our primary data set, we begin with households aged 65 or more in the 2004 HRS survey, and we collect information for these households back to the 1998 wave.[4] The advantage of using this "backward-looking" panel approach is that we condition on the survival of the household to 2004, and thus sidestep the potential for confounding survivorship bias in the 1998 cohort with household behavior.[5]

We begin with the RAND HRS data file, which is RAND's longitudinal file of commonly used HRS variables linked by households across time. We supplement this file with additional measures that we calculate from the HRS. Most importantly, we calculate the actuarial present value of expected flows from Social Security, defined-benefit pensions, life annuities, and transfer payments such as veterans' benefits, Food Stamps, and Supplemental Security Income. These calculations provide measures of annuity-like wealth that are often excluded from empirical analyses of portfolio and saving behavior.[6] With these variables included, we can analyze a comprehensive measure of wealth in order to learn how the various components and total resources are drawn down in retirement.

2.2. Characteristics of the Sample

Table 1 reports the age distribution for the sample we draw from the 2004 wave of the HRS; for couples, we report the age of the older member of the household. About half of our sample is under 75, and about half is older; married couples are much more likely to be in the younger group. Table 2 reports several other household characteristics describing our sample in 2004. Most single households are women (generally widows). Average annual income is about $44,000. Just over half of our sample have earned no more than a high school degree and fewer than one-fifth a college degree. About 1 in 10 households in our sample reports being nonwhite and about 1 in 20 being hispanic. More than a quarter of households include at least one person who perceives him or herself as being in either poor or fair health (as opposed to good or excellent health), and the average household spent about $6,700 out-of-pocket on medical care during the prior year.

Table 1. Age Distribution of Our Sample

Age in 2004	Sample Size	Weighted Percent	No. of Married Households	Weighted % Married
65-69	2,146	23.9	1,210	56.9
70-74	1,808	22.8	937	49.5
75-79	1,496	22.4	755	41.4
80-84	1,315	17.3	442	35.3
85-89	815	9.6	187	26.4
90 and over	478	4.0	67	18.0
Full Sample	8,058	100.0	3,598	43.6

Household observations drawn from the 2004 wave of the Health and Retirement Study (HRS).

Throughout the paper, "age" refers to the oldest person in the household.

Table 2. Household Characteristics

Variable	Mean
Age (years)	75.8
Married (%)	43.6
Single Male (%)	11.3
Single Female (%)	34.4
Income (thous. $2004)	43.8
Have Any Children (%)	93.5
Have Only a High School Degree (%)	53.2

Variable	Mean
Have a College Degree (%)	19.3
Nonwhite (%)	11.5
Hispanic (%)	4.9
Have a Person in Fair or Poor Health (%)	27.3
OOP Medical Expense (thous. $2004)	6.7

Household observations in 2004.
Means calculated using HRS sample weights.

Table 3. Components of Median Wealth: Households Aged 70 and Older in 2004*

	Thousands of 2004 $				Percent Share of Comp. Wealth in 2004
Component of Wealth	**1998**	**2000**	**2002**	**2004**	
Financial	87	90	77	74	22
Stocks[1]	35	38	31	29	9
Other[2]	51	52	47	45	14
Nonfinancial	115	113	110	111	34
Housing	84	84	87	89	27
Other[3]	31	29	24	22	7
Annuity-like benefits	217	193	169	143	44
Social Security	140	126	110	95	29
DB Pensions	63	55	47	38	12
Other[4]	14	12	11	10	3
Comprehensive Wealth	419	396	357	329	100
Number of Households	5,882	5,763	5,789	5,899	—

*The table reports means from subsamples selected to match the median of comprehensive wealth (CW) in the original sample, for each wave; thus, the components sum to median CW. Calculations use HRS sample weights.

[1] Includes shares held directly and indirectly through mutual funds, trusts, and retirement accounts.

[2] Includes liquid assets, bonds, and non-stock assets held in trusts and retirement accounts.

[3] Includes vehicles and businesses.

[4] Includes life annuities and government transfers.

2.3. The Composition and Level of Comprehensive Wealth in the HRS

Table 3 provides a breakdown of the components of comprehensive wealth for the median household aged 70 or older in 2004. The discounted present value of annuity-like benefits— Social Security, DB pensions, and other government transfers—accounted for about 44 percent of comprehensive wealth for the median household in 2004. By construction, the present value of these annuity-like streams decline as households age and their remaining life expectancies shrink. So, while we estimate a median annuity-like balance of $217,000 in 1998, by 2004 the value of this key source was just $143,000. Of course, this decline does not necessarily translate into a large drop in spendable resources *per year* because, as mentioned, remaining life expectancies decreased considerably over the six-year period as well.[7] For the median household in 2004, net nonfinancial wealth accounted for about one-third of comprehensive wealth ($111,000), with net housing wealth (home values net of mortgage debt) constituting the lion's share of this component ($89,000). Over the period from 1998 to 2004, the median balance of nonfinancial wealth fell only slightly (in real terms), as a small increase in the median household's net housing wealth was almost as large as the decline registered for the other components.[8] In 2004, just over one-fifth of the median household's comprehensive wealth was in the form of financial assets, and that year's balances were about 15 percent lower than in 1998 ($74,000 in 2004 vs. $87,000 in 1998).

Table 4 reports the evolution of comprehensive wealth from 1998 through 2004 for different types of households aged 70 and older in 2004. For the full sample, the real value of comprehensive wealth fell by 21 percent from 1998 through 2004. The rate of decline was larger for households older than age 80 (in 2004) than for those in their 70s and was much larger for single persons (around 28 percent) than for married couples (about 15 percent). In percentage terms, the net decrease in comprehensive wealth was smaller for households in the bottom quintile of the income distribution (11 percent from 1998 to 2004) and the top quintile (15 percent) than for middle-income retirees (21 percent).

Table 4. Evolution of Median Comprehensive Wealth[1] from 1998 to 2004: Households Aged 70 and Older in 2004

Thousands of 2004 $					
	1998	**2000**	**2002**	**2004**	**Cumulative Change, 1998 to 2004**
Full Sample	419	396	357	329	-21%
By Age in 2004:					
70-79	469	444	417	390	-17%
80-89	369	340	299	277	-25%
By Marital Status in 2004					
Single					
<=75	326	298	269	231	-29%
> 75	278	258	220	205	-26%
Married					
<=75	768	741	715	651	-15%
> 75	598	562	576	525	-12%
By Income in 2004[2]:					
Bottom 20%	164	161	155	146	-11%
Middle 60%	434	409	371	343	-21%
Top 20%	1018	978	887	863	-15%

[1]Comprehensive wealth is the sum of nancial, non nancial and annuity-like wealth. Medians are computed for each age-marital status-income cell.

[2] Income categories are de ned conditional on age and marital status in 1998.

3. A Measure of Annualized Wealth for Retirees

3.1. Definition of Annualized Wealth

The significant differences in comprehensive wealth by age and marital status highlight the importance of distinguishing between wealth *balances* and wealth *per person per expected* year of life, when considering the trajectory of resources in retirement. For this reason, we construct a measure of "annualized wealth" that indicates how much a household could, in principle, afford to spend per person per year over their remaining expected lifetimes, given their total resources (including current assets and future Social Security, pension, and welfare benefits). We demonstrate below that our measure is closely related to the optimal path of consumption in a simple life-cycle model and that it can also be derived from annuity-pricing principles.

For each household, we define annualized wealth as

$$AW_t = a_t W_t,$$

where W_t is a measure of a household's comprehensive wealth balances (or one of its major components—financial, nonfinancial, or annuity-like wealth) in period t, and a_t is the *per person* annualizing factor, defined as

$$a_t = \frac{r}{1+r}\left[\alpha - (\alpha-1)\frac{1}{(1+r)^{T_t^m}} - \frac{1}{(1+r)^{T_t^f}}\right]^{-1}, \tag{1}$$

where r is the real interest rate, α is an adjustment for household economies of scale that could reflect joint consumption possibilities (equal to 2 if there is no adjustment for economies of scale in consumption), and T_t^m and T_t^f indicate the two spouses' remaining life expectancies, assigned so that $T_t^m < T_t^f$.[9] Note that since T_t^m and T_t^f are age-dependent, the annualizing factor a_t is not constant over time.

To develop intuition about our measure of annualized wealth, it helps to consider some extreme values of the key parameters. For example, as the real interest rate approaches zero, the annualizing factor approaches

$$\frac{1}{(\alpha-1)T_t^m + T_t^f}.$$

Thus, ignoring household economies of scale (i.e., setting $\alpha = 2$), a zero interest rate implies that households can simply divide their total resources equally across the expected remaining years of life and consume that amount per person each year. With economies of scale (i.e., $\alpha < 2$), annualized wealth is larger because both members are alive for the first T_t^m years, during which time they can consume more efficiently together (allowing a given stock of wealth to "last longer").

To take another extreme case, consider what happens to the annualizing factor if each member of the household were to expect to live forever. In this case, $T_t^m = T_t^f = \infty$ and the factor approaches

$$\frac{r}{1+r}\left[1-\frac{1}{(1+r)^{T_t^f}}\right]^{-1}.$$

which implies that each year the household can afford to consume no more than its annual interest income r.[10] Table 5 illustrates some additional examples of the values of annualized wealth that would result from a $100,000 wealth position, given different assumptions about interest rates and life expectancies. The top row shows that when a single individual expects to live just one more year, then, regardless of the interest rate, annualized wealth is the full $100,000. This also equals the optimal amount of consumption in a life cycle model with certain longevity and no bequests or random medical expenses. The remaining entries in the table demonstrate the intuitive result that annualized wealth declines with life expectancy and rises with the real interest rate. For instance, for our baseline interest rate assumption of 2.5%, we see that doubling the expected lifespans of each member from 10 years to 20 years would decrease the annualized value of $100,000 by 44 percent, from $5,600 per person per year to $3,100 per person per year.

As we will show next, our measure of annualized wealth is closely related to two common concepts in economics—optimal consumption according to Modigliani's life cycle hypothesis and the annual payment that could be received from an actuarially fair, real, joint fixed life annuity that might be purchased (in principle) with a household's comprehensive wealth.

Table 5. Examples of Annualized Wealth from $ 100K of Total Wealth

		Real Interest Rate *r*		
T^m	T^f	**0%**	**2.5%**	**5.0%**
0	1	100.0	100.0	100.0
	10	10.0	11.2	12.3
	20	5.0	6.3	7.6
10	1	9.2	10.0	11.0
	10	5.0	5.6	6.2
	20	3.3	4.0	4.7
20	1	4.8	5.9	7.1
	10	3.3	4.0	4.7
	20	2.5	3.1	3.8

Annualized wealth in thousands of dollars. T^m and T^f denote the expected remaining life years for the spouses.

3.2. Annualized Wealth and the Life Cycle Model

Consider the optimal consumption problem facing a representative household consisting of two members, who differ only in their probabilities of survival. Conditional on being alive in period 0, each member lives to period t with cumulative probability S_t^m and S_t^f, respectively, with terminal probabilities $S_T^m = S_T^f = 0$. They start the period with comprehensive wealth position of W_0, which is the sum of their net worth from financial and nonfinancial assets and the present discounted value of any annuity streams (such as Social Security and DB pension benefits). According to the life cycle hypothesis, the household is assumed to maximize

$$U_0 = \sum_{t=0}^{T} \beta^t \left\{ S_t^f S_t^m \alpha u\left(\frac{C_t}{\alpha}\right) + [S_t^f(1 - S_t^m) + S_t^m(1 - S_t^f)]u(C_t) \right\}, \tag{2}$$

Subject to the lifetime resource constraint

$$\sum_{t=0}^{T} \frac{C_t}{(1+r)^t} = W_0, \tag{3}$$

where α captures the possibility of economies of scale from joint consumption within the household, β is the discount factor, r is the real interest rate, and within-period utility is given by the function $u(.)$. For now, we assume that $u(.)$ = ln(.) and that the discount factor and the interest rate offset one another, so that $(1 + r)\beta = 1$.

Rearranging the resulting Euler equation for this constrained optimization problem, consumption can be shown to grow according to

$$\frac{C_{t+1}}{C_t} = \frac{\Psi_{t+1}}{\Psi_t},$$

where

$$\Psi_t = S_t^f S_t^m \alpha + S_t^f(1 - S_t^m) + S_t^m(1 - S_t^f).$$

If both members of the household are alive in period 0, $\psi_0=\alpha$. Therelationship between consumption in period 0 and expected consumption in some future period t is then given by

$$C_t = \frac{\Psi_t}{\alpha} C_0. \tag{4}$$

Substituting this expression into the resource constraint and expanding ψ_t we can solve for first period consumption as

$$C_0 \sum_{t=0}^{T} \left\{ \frac{S_t^f S_t^m + \frac{1}{\alpha}[S_t^f(1-S_t^m) + S_t^m(1-S_t^f)]}{(1+r)^t} \right\} = W_0, \tag{5}$$

which we will see is identical to the formula for an actuarially-fair joint life annuity that pays C_0 when both members are alive, and C_0/α when only one member is alive. To simplify the problem, assume that the first member of the household lives T^f periods with certainty and the second member lives $T^m < T^f$ periods with certainty. Applying the formula for a finite sum, we can write equation (5) as

$$C_0 \frac{1+r}{r} \left[1 - \left(1 - \frac{1}{\alpha}\right) \frac{1}{(1+r)^{T^m}} - \frac{1}{(1+r)^{T^f} \alpha} \right] = W_0. \tag{6}$$

Annual consumption per person, C_0/α, adjusted for household economies of scale, is then given by

$$C_0/\alpha = aW_0,$$

where a is the annualizing factor defined in equation (1).

The fact that our annualized wealth measure can be derived from a standard life cycle model suggests that it bears a close resemblance to the notion of permanent income that is fundamental in most analysis of consumption and savings. When we apply the measure to the data, however, we should keep in mind that annualized wealth only equals permanent income in the special case of: (1) zero utility from bequests, (2) $\beta(1 + r) = 1$, and (3) log utility over annual consumption. In general, annualized wealth will not equal optimal consumption. For example, in the presence of bequests or uncertain medical expenses, we would expect households to dissave at a slower rate than the simple life cycle model would predict. In Section 6, we investigate these issues in detail by simulating expanded life cycle models that include random medical expenses and explicit bequest motives and compare the empirical trajectories of annualized wealth in the HRS with optimal paths from those model specifications.

3.3. Annualized Wealth and Joint Life Annuities

We now demonstrate that our measure of annualized wealth is closely related to an actuarially fair, inflation-indexed, joint fixed life annuity that a retired household could theoretically purchase with all of its assets.[11] Brown and Poterba (2000)) show that, using the "last survivor payout rule," the actuarially fair price of a fixed joint annuity paying a real amount \$1 each year that both members of a household are alive and an amount \$A each year that only one member is alive is given by

$$p = \sum_{t=0}^{T} \left\{ \frac{S_t^f S_t^m + \lambda[S_t^f(1 - S_t^m) + S_t^m(1 - S_t^f)]}{(1 + r)^t} \right\},$$

where T is the maximum lifespan for either member, r is the real interest rate, and S_t^m and S_t^f denote the cumulative survival probabilities for the husband and wife.[12] It follows that if a household were to use its entire balance of comprehensive wealth (W_0) to purchase this actuarially fair annuity, it could receive annual payments of W_0/p.[13] This annuity would allow the household to consume $C_0 = W_0/p$, which is the same expression as equation (5), as long as λ is set equal to $1/\alpha$.

Put another way, simple life cycle theory implies that (in the absence of bequests or precautionary saving), households would optimally fully annuitize their wealth and set annual consumption equal to the annuity receipt. However, in the expanded life cycle models we investigate in Section 6—

which include explicit bequest motives and random medical expenses—full annuitization is not optimal (even if actuarially fair annuities were to exist).

3.4. Discussion of Annualized Wealth

We have shown that our measure of annualized wealth is closely related to optimal consumption behavior according to a stylized life cycle model, and can also be thought of as the value of an actuarially fair, real fixed annuity that a retired household could, in principle, afford to purchase with its total resources. Each angle provides a different perspective on the empirical application of our measure. What does it mean when we observe that a household in the HRS has, say, $20,000 in annualized wealth? Viewed through the lens of the life cycle model, we can say that the $20,000 corresponds loosely to each household member's permanent income, and, for certain parameterizations, to its optimal choice of consumption (per person). Viewed as an actuarially fair annuity, the measure tells us that each member of the household has enough resources to afford to purchase a real, joint life annuity that pays $20,000 per person per year, fully insulating their consumption possibilities from randomness over how long they will actually live.

3.5. Annualized Wealth in the HRS

Table 6 reports the components of annualized comprehensive wealth from 1998 through 2004 for the median household aged 70 or older in 2004. At the median, annualized comprehensive wealth was $28,100 in 2004, 13 percent more than the median value in 1998 ($24,900). From 1998 to 2004, the contribution of annuity-like benefits to annualized comprehensive wealth declined slightly, from $12,800 to $12,100, likely due to the non-indexation of some DB payments. However, the decline in annuity-like wealth was more than offset by increases in the annualized value of financial assets (from $5,200 per person per expected year to $6,400) and nonfinancial wealth (from $6,900 to $9,400). Median annualized net housing wealth rose 51% from $5,100 in 1998 to $7,700 in 2004. This relatively large increase was accounted for by a net increase in actual wealth (from a balance of $84,000 in 1998 to $89,000 in 2004) combined with shorter remaining life expectancies (and, thus, smaller annualizing factors) as the median household aged. By contrast, the smaller net rise in annualized financial assets from 1998 to 2004 was accounted for by a decline in actual wealth (from $87,000 to $74,000) that was slow relative to the drop in the median household's remaining life expectancy.

That median annualized comprehensive wealth generally rose between the 1998 and 2004 waves of the HRS is one of the primary results in our paper. Clearly, part of the story for rising annualized wealth was that retirees accrued capital gains on their homes. But, retirees evidently did not offset those gains by rapidly spending down either their financial or nonfinancial assets.

Table 6. Components of Median Annualized Comprehensive Wealth: Households Aged 70 and Older 2004*

Thousands of 2004 $ per person per year					
Component of Wealth	**1998**	**2000**	**2002**	**2004**	**Cumulative Change, 1998 to 2004**
Financial	5.2	5.9	5.9	6.4	23%
Stocks[1]	2.1	2.4	2.3	2.4	14%
Other[2]	3.1	3.5	3.6	4.0	29%
Nonfinancial	6.9	7.5	8.5	9.4	36%
Housing	5.1	5.7	6.7	7.7	51%
Other[3]	1.7	1.8	1.8	1.7	0%
Annuity-like benefits	12.8	12.6	12.6	12.3	-4%
Social Security	8.3	8.3	8.3	8.1	-3%
DB Pensions	3.7	3.5	3.5	3.3	-11%
Other[4]	0.8	0.8	0.9	0.9	13%
Comprehensive Wealth	24.9	25.9	27.0	28.1	13%
Number of Households	5,882	5,763	5,789	5,899	—

[1] Annualized wealth is wealth per person per expected year of life, in thousands of 2004 dollars (see text for details).

[2] Table reports means from subsamples selected to match median annualized comprehensive wealth (ACW) in the original sample, for each household type and each wave, so that the components sum to median ACW. Calculations use HRS sample weights.

Table 7. Evolution of Median Annualized Comprehensive Wealth from 1998 to 2004: Households Aged 70 and Older in 2004.

Thousands of 2004 $ per person per year					
Classification	**1998**	**2000**	**2002**	**2004**	**Cumulative Change, 1998 to 2004**
Full Sample	24.9	25.9	27.0	28.1	13%
By Age in 2004:					
70-79	23.2	23.9	24.8	25.4	9%
80-89	27.6	28.3	30.9	32.6	18%
By Marital Status in 2004					
Single					
<=75	19.8	20.2	20.5	21.2	7%
> 75	25.0	26.5	26.8	29.4	18%
Married (α =2)[1]					
<=75	27.3	26.8	27.5	27.3	0%
> 75	29.0	29.5	32.1	32.4	12%
Married (α =1.67)[1]					
<=75	32.3	32.2	33.0	33.2	3%
> 75	34.0	34.7	38.5	39.0	15%
By Income in 2004[2] :					
Bottom 20%	10.8	11.0	11.4	11.4	6%
Middle 60%	24.7	25.9	26.7	27.8	13%
Top 20%	58.2	60.4	64.2	69.5	19%

[1] α measures household economies of scale: α=2 implies no scale economies, while α =1.67 implies a measure of scale economies sometimes used in the literature (see text for details).

[2] Income categories are defined conditional on age and marital status in 1998.

Table 7 breaks down the evolution of annualized comprehensive wealth between 1998 and 2004 for the median household of different ages, family compositions, and income levels. Annualized wealth rose even faster for older retirees (aged 80-89) than younger retirees (aged 70-79). Among single retirees in 2004, annualized wealth rose in both age groups, while among married retirees in 2004, only the older cohort experienced an increase. As can be seen in the middle of the table, the time-path of annualized comprehensive wealth appears to be little affected by accounting for economies of scale in household consumption. Perhaps surprisingly, we find increases in annualized comprehensive wealth for the median household in each of the three income groups shown in the table. Among those in the bottom quintile of the income distribution in 2004, annualized comprehensive wealth increased 6 percent between 1998 and 2004. The rises were larger for middle-income retirees (13 percent) and those in the upper income quintile (19 percent).

Table 8 reports the frequency distribution of percentage changes in annualized comprehensive wealth for different types of households. Across the entire sample, the table shows that 48 percent of of retirees aged 70 and older (in 2004) experienced increases of at least 10 percent, while 30 percent experienced decreases of at least 10 percent over that time period. The table shows that the frequency distribution of changes in annualized wealth was essentially the same across age and marital status groups in 2004. We find small differences in the right tails across the three income groups—the share of households in the upper income quintile that experienced a 10 percent or larger increase is 50 percent, while the share is 46 percent among middle-income retirees and 42 percent for those in the bottom income quintile. Nonetheless, these distributions are remarkably stable across age, marital status, and income groups: In particular, in every row of Table 8, the greatest frequency of HRS households experienced an *increase* in annualized comprehensive wealth of 25 percent or more from 1998 through 2004.

4. Nonparametric Age Profiles of Comprehensive Wealth in the HRS

4.1. Methodology

As a preliminary look at the evolution of resources over the course of retirement, we construct nonparametric profiles of median wealth between ages 60 and 90 years.[14] To produce these profiles, we divide the sample into 3-year age bins in 1998 and calculate the median value of wealth for each bin over the following six years.[15] We plot four points for each age group, corresponding to the 1998, 2000, 2002 and 2004 waves of the HRS. Arrayed by age on the horizontal axis, the series of segments trace out an empirical age profile of wealth.

Table 8. Distribution of Cumulative Changes in Annualized Comprehensive Wealth from 1998 to 2004: Households 70 and Older in 2004

Classification	Percent of Households with a Change in Annualized Comprehensive Wealth that is:				
	<-25%	-25% to -10%	-10% to 10%	10% to 25%	>25%
Full Sample	17	13	22	13	35
By Age in 2004:					
70-79	17	14	23	14	33
80-89	17	11	22	11	38
By Marital Status in 2004					
Single					
<=75	19	13	22	12	34
>75	18	11	21	12	39
Married (α =2)[1]					
<=75	17	16	23	15	29
>75	16	11	25	14	34
Married (α =1.67)[1]					
<=75	16	17	23	15	30
>75	16	11	25	14	34
By Income in 2004[2]:					
Bottom 20%	17	13	29	12	30
Middle 60%	17	13	23	13	33
Top 20%	19	13	18	12	38

[1] α measures household economies of scale: α =2 implies no scale economies, while α =1.67 implies a measure of scale economies sometimes used in the literature (see text for details).

[2] Income categories are defined conditional on age and marital status in 2004

Note that to interpret the resulting graph as an age profile, one must ignore the effects of cohort differences between the segments.[16] In addition to cohort effects, another issue of concern is survivorship bias: since lower-wealth households are more likely to die in any given year than higher-wealth households, the slope of any given wealth segment is likely to be biased upward (i.e., more positive or less negative) relative to what would be the case without such truncation. This is an issue that we will address, at least partially, in the next section when we develop a regression-based methodology for estimating age profiles of wealth that uses the panel nature of the HRS data explicitly.

4.2. Results

Figure 1 displays median age profiles of comprehensive wealth balances (not annualized, not per person) and each of its major components (in thousands of 2004 dollars). Beginning with the top left panel, we can see that median financial wealth declines quite gradually over the retirement period—from about $70,000 at age 62 to about $20,000 by age 90 (abstracting from the relatively small cohort differences in the levels of the line segments). Nonfinancial wealth is flat at around $100,000 from age 62 until almost age 85 and it falls, on balance, at the later ages. The profile of annuity-like wealth shows a prominent peak around age 62, when Social Security benefits first come available, followed by a steady and substantial decline. This effect is more mechanical than behavioral: the present value spikes as the onset of payments approaches, then declines with life expectancy. Summing the three major components, we find that median comprehensive wealth peaks at about $500,000 around age 62 and drops to below $200,000 by the late 80s. Still, the median retiree in the HRS continues to hold a significant amount of wealth even at rather advanced ages.

The declining profiles of wealth at older ages suggests that some degree of spend-down is occurring. To learn more about the implications of this spend-down for individual resources, we turn to our concept of annualized wealth. Figure 2 shows that median annualized financial wealth is flat or rising a bit over the entire age range. This suggests that households do not appear to run down their financial wealth any more quickly than their life expectancies are shortening. We also see an increase in annualized nonfinancial wealth, suggesting that households may indeed be reluctant to fully consume their housing wealth as they age. The annualized value of annuity-like wealth is roughly flat after age 62, with perhaps a slight decline due to non-indexation of some benefits. When summed together, median annualized comprehensive wealth shows a gentle upward slope across older ages, so that, all told, the median value rises from about $17,000 per person per year at age 62 to about $30,000 per person per year at age 90.

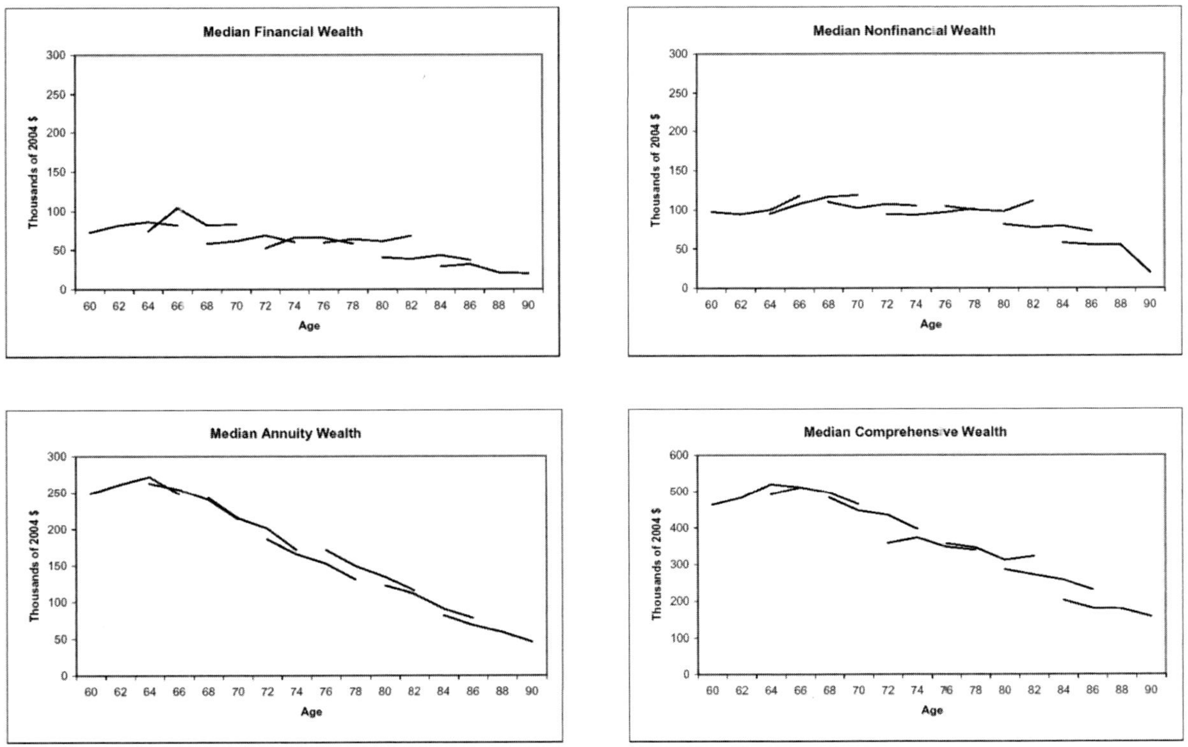

Figure 1. NonparametricAgeProfilesofMedianWealth:RawData

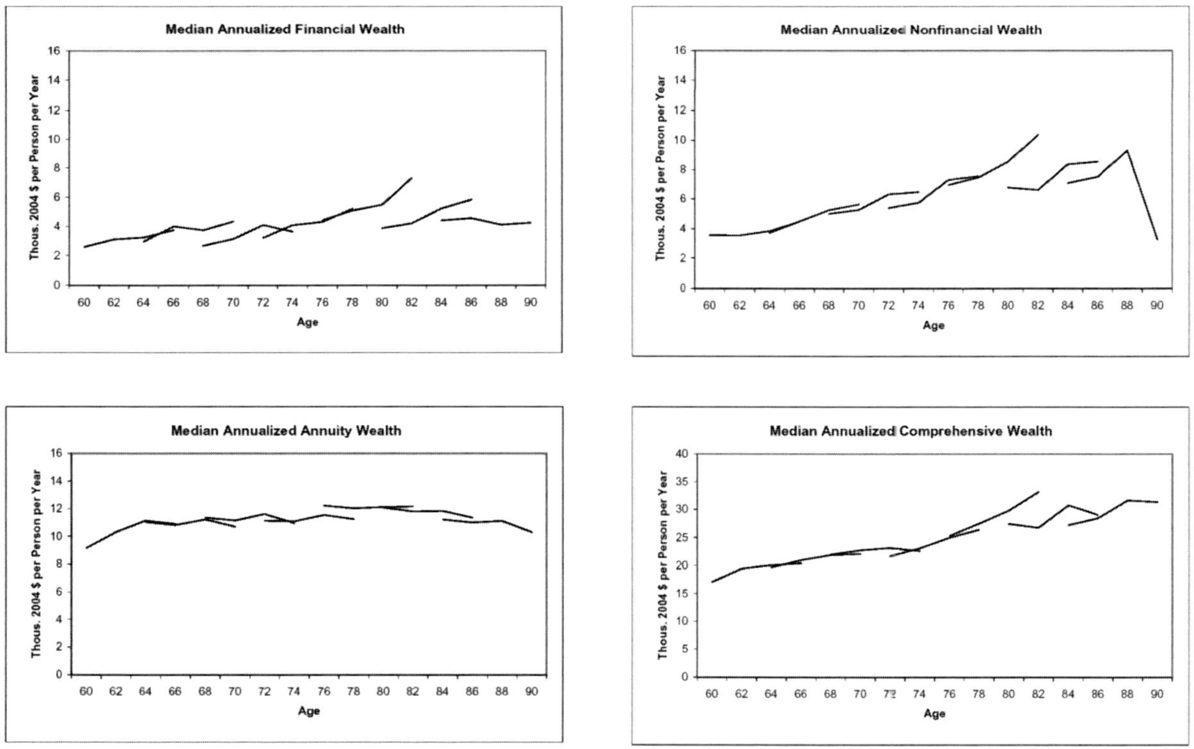

Figure 2. Nonparametric Age Profiles of Median Annualized Wealth: Raw Data

5. Regression-Based Age Profiles of Comprehensive Wealth in the HRS

5.1. Methodology

A natural concern regarding the nonparametric wealth profiles just discussed is that they are susceptible to survivorship bias and, in addition, make no attempt to control for the effects that a variety of observable factors have on the rate of change of household wealth in retirement. In this section, we present regression-based age profiles for comprehensive wealth that address these issues by using the full extent of the panel data in the HRS.

For each major component of comprehensive wealth, and for each income group[17], we use a four-step procedure to estimate age-profiles. First, we calculate a household-level growth factor from each wave to the next (that is, three growth factors per household). Second, we pool all of the growth factors and estimate a median regression of the growth factors on a set of household characteristics, including indicators for two-year age brackets (e.g., 60-61, 62-63, etc.), survey-year dummies, and a range of other characteristics.[18] Third, we use the estimated coefficients on the age indicators to calculate predicted median growth factors for each age-group and multiply these together to construct a "cumulative growth factor" across the full range of ages.[19] Finally, we "connect the dots" between the predicted cumulative growth factors to form a regression-based age profile. The resulting profile will be purely relative (e.g., an index starting from one at age 60); to convert it to level terms, we benchmark the middle of each age profile so that it passes through the median level of wealth held by 75-year olds in 2004.

5.2. Results

Figure 3 shows that the regression-based age profiles are generally similar to the nonparametric profiles presented above. For retirees in the bottom income quintile, median financial wealth is essentially zero at all ages, while for those in the middle part of the income distribution, median financial wealth stays near $60,000 from age 62 to almost age 80, and then declines to about $30,000 over the next 10 years of retirement. Among upper-income households, median financial wealth stays pretty close to $250,000 from age 62 to almost age 80, and then it falls to about $125,000 by age 90.

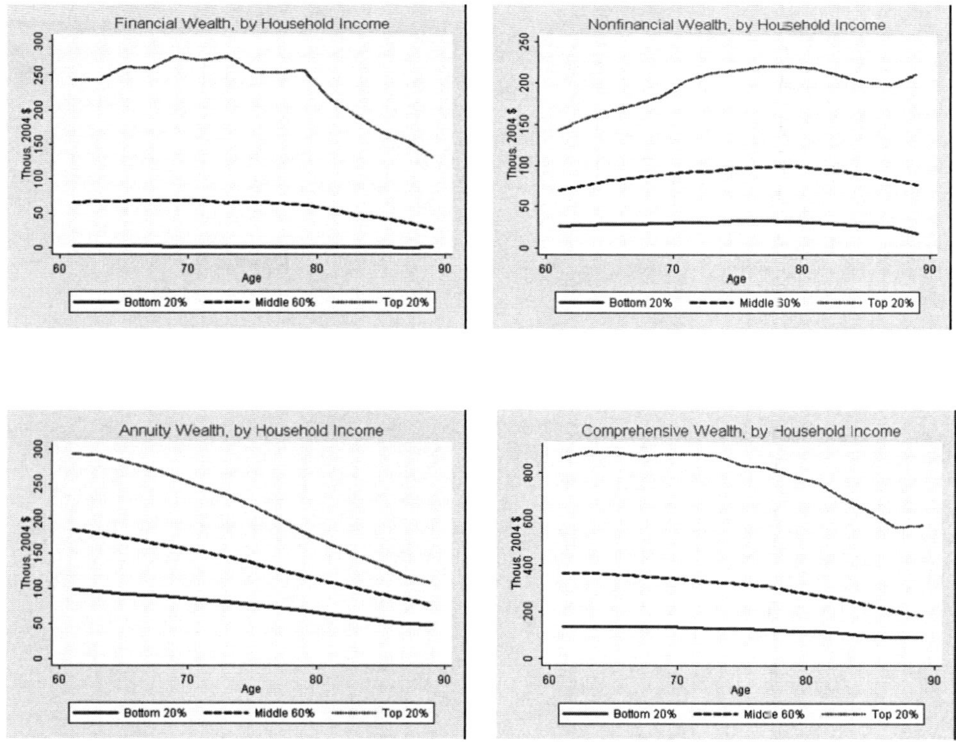

Figure 3. Regression-Based Age Profiles of Median Wealth Balances, by Household Income

Median nonfinancial wealth, for all three of the income groups, exhibits a slight hump shape that peaks around age 75. Thus, households in the bottom and middle quintiles of the income distribution (conditional on age and marital status) have about the same level of nonfinancial wealth in their mid-60s as they have in their mid-80s—$25,000 for the lower-income households, and $75,000 for the median income group. In the upper quintile of the income distribution, though, we estimate that despite the hump, nonfinancial wealth tends to rise a little over the course of retirement, from nearly $175,000 at the median in the mid-60s to about $200,000 by the mid-80s.

As we would expect, the present discounted value of annuity-like wealth falls steadily and substantially in retirement—for all three income groups, the median balance is about half as large around age 85 as it was around age 65. As with the nonparametric age profiles, the downward-sloping trajectory of annuity-like balances is mainly a mechanical result of shorter remaining lifespans.

Putting the major components together, the lower right panel of figure 3 shows that for retirees in all three income groups, median comprehensive wealth is fairly flat between ages 62 and 75. In the latter 70s and in the 80s, though, balances decrease more noticeably with age, particularly for households in the middle- and upper-income groups.[20]

Figure 4 shows the regression-based age profiles for annualized comprehensive wealth and its components. Again, these profiles are quite similar to those generated nonparametrically.

It seems quite clear that households in the bottom income quintile are not relying on financial assets to finance spending in retirement—median annualized financial wealth stays at zero for this group at all ages in the HRS. However, for the middle-income retirees, median financial assets contribute about $5,000 per person per year to comprehensive wealth and, strikingly, this level does not fall over the course of retirement. Indeed, there is a very slight increase in annualized financial wealth through age 80 for the middle-income group. For households in the upper quintile of income, median annualized financial wealth shows a more pronounced increase from the early 60s (about $20,000 per person per year) through the late 70s (about $25,000); then it stays about flat for retirees in their 80s. Median nonfinancial wealth increases in annualized terms for all three income groups. While the levels are very different across the three income groups, all three groups nearly double their annualized nonfinancial wealth between the mid-60s and the mid-80s.

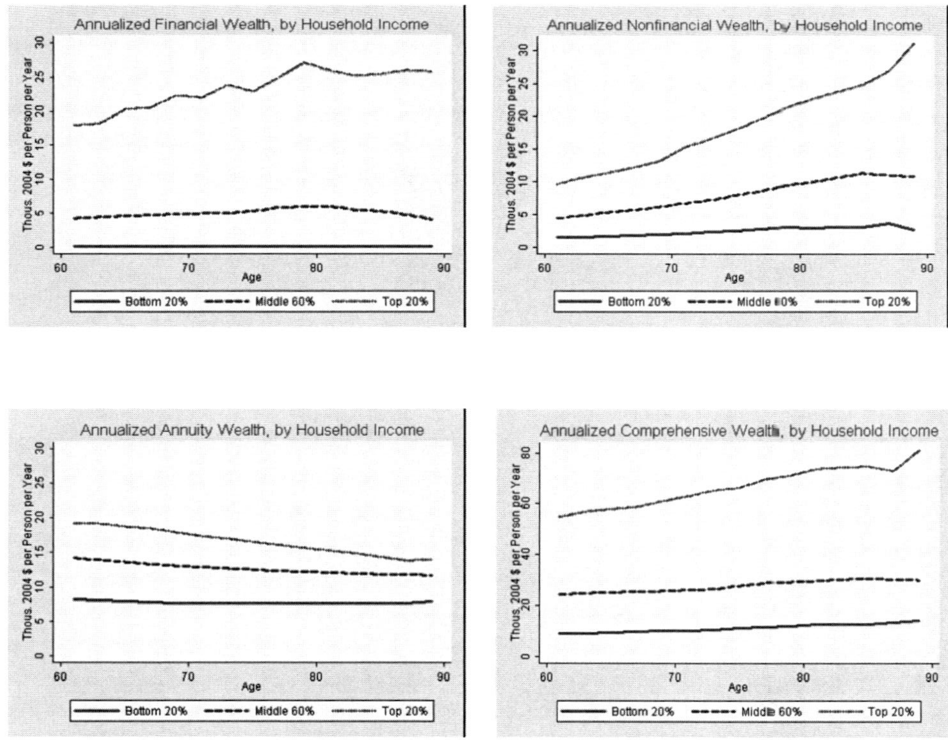

Figure 4. Regression-Based Age Profiles of Median Annualized Wealth, by Household Income

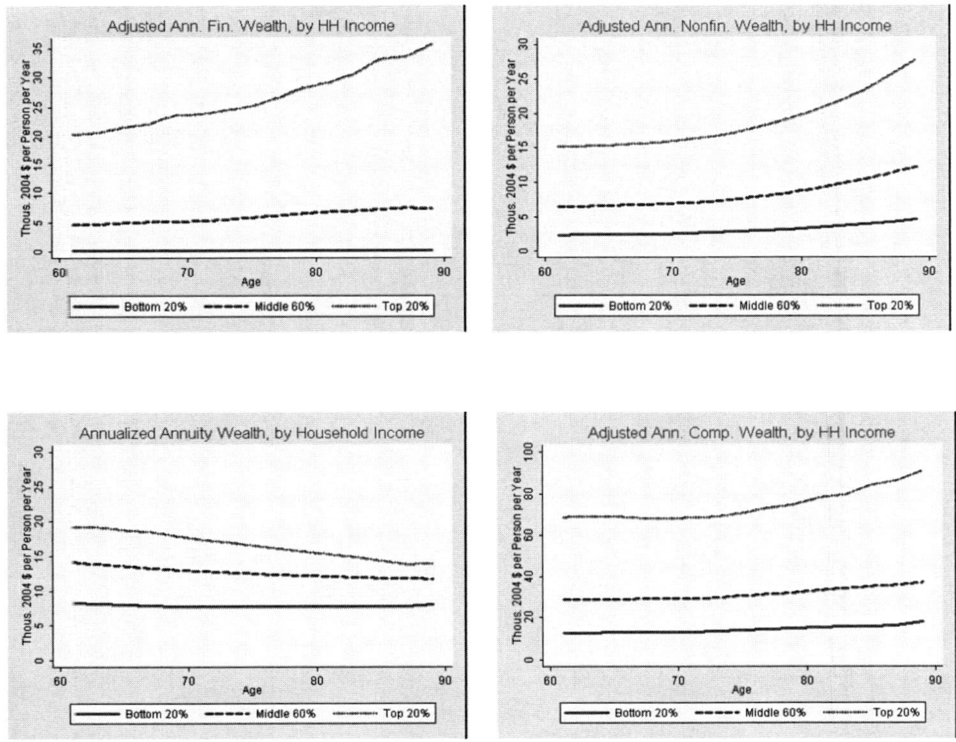

Figure 5. Regression-Based Age Profiles of Median AnnualizedWealth Excluding Capital Gains on Corporate Equity and Housing, by Household Income

The median level of annualized annuity-like wealth is essentially flat for lower- and middle-income households from the mid-60s through the late-80s—at about $8,000 and $14,000 per person per year, respectively—while the upper-income quintile experiences a significant decrease over the course of retirement—from almost $20,000 per person per year in their mid-60s to about $15,000 by their late-80s. This is mainly a result of reduced wealth, in real per person terms, from private DB pension benefits as retirees age.[21] Turning to the age profiles in the lower right panel, we find that, all told, between the early and the late retirement years, median annualized comprehensive wealth shows a mild net increase for lower- and middle-income households, and a pronounced rise for upper-income households.

5.3. The Effect of Capital Gains on the Estimated Age Profiles

How should we interpret this build-up in wealth relative to life expectancy at the end of the life cycle? Before considering explanations from the perspective of a life cycle framework, we first ask whether the upward-sloping age profiles for annualized comprehensive wealth in the HRS are simply the consequence of unexpected capital gains on housing or corporate equity over the 1998-2004 sample period. To answer this question, we re-estimate the regression- based age profiles using a counterfactual HRS dataset that holds each household's level of corporate equity and net housing wealth fixed over the sample years, letting the other components of comprehensive wealth follow their reported trajectories in the HRS.

Because equity prices gyrated markedly over the 1998-2004 period, we compute counterfactual trajectories in the HRS panel data by replacing each household's reported holdings of corporate equity in each wave with its (household-specific) average value over the six-year period.[22] Similarly, because average home prices around the country climbed substantially between 1998 and 2004, we replace each household's reported housing wealth in the four waves with the level it reported in 1998 (thereby assuming no change in housing wealth over our sample period).[23]

Figure 5 shows that making these adjustments to the reported measures of comprehensive wealth in the HRS do not materially change our finding that, in annualized terms, median tends to rise with age during retirement for the median household in all three income groups. If anything, the profile of annualized financial wealth appears to rise slightly more after the adjustment, and both nonfinancial and comprehensive wealth continue to show clearly rising profiles. The upward sloping (regression-based) age profiles in our counterfactual measures shows that, over the sample period, other forms of financial and nonfinancial wealth (such as deposits, money market funds, mutual funds, vehicles, and business equity) increased notably in annualized terms across waves of the HRS. But more importantly, the rising slope *across* cohorts reflects different starting levels of wealth by age as of the base year of 1998.[24] Thus, we do not think that the upward sloping age profile for annualized comprehensive wealth over retirement is being driven primarily by the effects of unanticipated capital gains on corporate equity or housing over the specific sample period that is available.

6. Predicted Age Profiles for Annualized Comprehensive Wealth from Life Cycle Model Simulations

In this section, we ask whether the pattern of rising annualized wealth at the median can be explained using fairly standard extensions to the life cycle model of consumption. In Section 3 we showed that the simplest life cycle model predicts that annualized wealth should be roughly constant in retirement. The question we turn to now is whether adding plausible bequest or precautionary motives to the life cycle model can generate upward- sloping profiles for annualized wealth that resemble those in the HRS. We adopt a modeling framework that is simple enough to illustrate the key forces that could shape the empirical patterns, but sufficiently rich to quantify realistic influences on savings behavior.[25] We consider a range of fairly standard model specifications,[26] but our search is by no means exhaustive.

6.1. Description of the Models We Consider

We consider models in which retired households maximize the expected discounted utility from consumption from their current age t to a maximum age T subject to a budget constraint that represents a transition equation for wealth X_t (more accurately, cash-onhand) and a non-negativity constraint for wealth at each age.[27] Households are assumed to maximize lifetime utility given by

$$V(X_t, n_t) = \max_{C_t} \left[\alpha(n_t) U\left(C_t, \alpha(n_t)\right) + \beta \sum_{j=1}^{3} \psi_{t+1,j} E_t V(X_{t+1}, n_j) + \beta(1 - \sum_{j=1}^{3} \psi_{t+1,j}) B(X_{t+1}) \right], \tag{7}$$

subject to

$$X_{t+1} = \max[R(X_t - C_t) + Y_{t+1} - M_{t+1}, F] \tag{8}$$

$$C_t \leq X_t, \tag{9}$$

where E_t denotes expectations over uncertain medical expenses and mortality, $B(.)$ is a bequest function that equals zero if any member of the household is alive, and $\psi_{t+1,j}$ represents the probability associated with each of three states of the world in the following period: both spouses survive, only the husband survives, or only the wife survives. In the budget constraint, Y_t is retirement income, M_t are out-of-pocket medical expenses, and F is a consumption floor that we assume can always be financed (e.g., by welfare or other government transfers).

We assume utility over consumption takes the iso-elastic form, $U(C_t, n_t) = \frac{(C_t/\alpha(n_t))^{1-\sigma}}{1-\sigma}$. In our framework, n_t is a state variable indicating a household's demographic structure: for couples, $n_t = 1$, for single men, $n_t = 2$, and for single women, $n_t = 3$. The function $\alpha(n_t)$ is used to capture economies of scale for couples in household production (specifically, $\alpha(n_t = 1) = 1.67$ and $\alpha\ (n_t = \{2, 3\}) = 1$). In some specifications, we ignore possible economies of scale, setting $\alpha = 1$ for all n_t. In all specifications discussed in this paper, we set the preference parameter σ to 3.[28] In the transition equation for wealth, (8), we use $R = 1.025$—the same value we used in our present value calculations with the HRS data. For each income group, we set Y_t to match the median level of annuity income (essentially Social Security and DB pension benefits) in the HRS. We report the full set of parameters in Table 9.

In some versions of the life cycle model, we assume that households explicitly derive utility from leaving a bequest upon their death, according to the iso-elastic utility function:

Table 9. Parameter Values in Life Cycle Simulation.

Parameter	Value	Definition
T	109	maximum age
β	0.976	discount factor
R	1.025	gross real interest rate
σ	3	coefficient of relative risk aversion
α	1.67	household equivalence scale
b_1	0.05	bequest function parameter
b_2	5,000	bequest function parameter
F	2,000-4,000	consumption floor
σ_ζ^2	0.909	variance of the AR1 shock to medical costs
σ_ε^2	1.819	variance of the transitory shock to medical costs
η	0.925	correlation on the AR1 component of medical costs
μ	0.75	fraction of married household medical costs paid by singles
Y_t^s	20.0, 11.5, 6.8	income (in 1,000s) for high, medium, and low education single
Y_t^m	35.0, 26.0, 16.0	income (in \$1,000s) for high, medium, and low education married couples
X_0^s	275.5, 89.2, 1.9	initial cash on hand (in 1,000s) for high, medium, and low education single
X_0^m	671.4, 271.0, 71.3	initial cash on hand (in \$1,000s) for high, medium, and low education married couples

$$B(X_t) = \frac{(b_1 X_t + b_2)^{1-\sigma}}{1-\sigma}. \tag{10}$$

In this set-up, the parameter b_1 is like an annuity factor that converts a lump sum bequest in the amount of X_t to the annual consumption flow it could afford. In the simulations, we set $b_1 = .05$ so that intended bequests are assumed to generate a flow of utility that relates to approximately twenty-years worth of their heirs' consumption. We set the "shift" parameter $b_2 = 5{,}000$ so that, in the model, retirees without many resources will not face a strong incentive to leave a sizable bequest. In equation (10), we set $\sigma = 3$, so that the same parameter value governs both the shape of the bequest function (conditional on b_1 and b_2) and the shape of the utility function over consumption (conditional on $\alpha(n_t)$).[29]

In the extended life cycle model, the variable M_{t+1} denotes a random draw for out- of-pocket medical expenses, which will induce a precautionary motive for retirees to hold wealth balances into old age. Our parameterization for M_{t+1} matches the econometric estimates that French and Jones (2004b) produced using panel data from the AHEAD sample. In their econometric model—

which is able to match many key features of the micro-data—medical expenses are assumed to have a trend component that is increasing with age (t) and income (Y_t) and a stochastic component that is the sum of a persistent shock (AR(1)) and a transitory shock. The parameter F and the non-negativity constraint (9) place a lower bound on utility in case a realization of out-of-pocket medical expenses exceeds a household's wealth.[30]

Following French (2005), the natural logarithm of out-of-pocket medical expenses, M_t, evolves according to:

$$\begin{aligned} \ln M_{t+1} &= \mu_{t+1} + \eta_{t+1} + \varepsilon_{t+1} \\ \eta_{t+1} &= \rho\eta_t + \zeta_{t+1}, \end{aligned}$$

where μ_t is an age-specific trend, η_t is an autoregressive component, and ε_t is a transitory component. The trend of log medical expenses evolves as follows:

$$\mu_t = \mu_0 + \mu_1(t - \bar{t}) + \mu_2(t - \bar{t})^2,$$

where μ_0, μ_1 and μ_2 are the coefficient estimates from French and Jones (2004b) and $\bar{t}$ denotes the average age in their sample. Following the method in Tauchen and Hussey (1991), we approximate the persistent component η_t with a four-state Markov chain and the transitory shock ε_t using five-point Gauss-Hermite quadrature.

Our specification of medical expenditures seems to fit the AHEAD data fairly well (see French and Jones, 2004b), but it may understate the strength of the relationship between income or wealth and medical expenses. If so, our model may attribute too much of the observed rise in annualized resources among wealthier households to a strong bequest motive, operating through $B(X_t)$, rather than a tendency for higher-income retirees to plan to spend significantly more on medical care in old age relative to lower-income households.

Table 10. Comparison of Life-Cycle Models and Data*

Age and Household Type	HRS[1]	Model A[2]	Model B[3]	Model C[4]	Model D[5]	Model E[6]	Model F[7]
Singles:							
65-70	19.60	20.92	21.15	21.30	21.55	21.84	21.89
75-80	25.20	22.90	25.23	25.70	26.75	29.03	29.85
85-90	27.70	20.17	27.12	26.36	29.79	33.45	36.36
Married (without scales):							
65-70	25.40	25.23	25.40	25.78	25.85	25.99	26.03
75-80	27.90	23.73	25.09	27.05	27.55	28.63	28.93
85-90	39.30	19.90	23.70	27.05	28.69	31.55	32.60
Married (scales: $\alpha = 1.67$):							
65-70	30.60	30.55	30.82	31.17	31.27	31.41	31.48
75-80	33.30	30.10	32.06	33.69	34.51	35.51	35.97
85-90	45.60	27.47	33.46	35.57	38.20	40.99	42.54
Full sample:							
65-70	22.50	22.71	22.93	23.24	23.35	23.62	23.64
75-80	26.60	23.11	25.15	26.03	27.04	29.10	29.64
85-90	29.00	20.18	26.91	26.34	29.78	33.48	35.98

*Annualized wealth in thousands of 2004 dollars. See text for details. The coefficient of relative risk aversion $\sigma = 3$, the bequest function is given by equation (10), and F is the value of the consumption floor.

[1]Median annualized wealth for pooled 1998-2004 sample in HRS.

[2] Model A: survival uncertainty with no bequests.

[3] Model B: survival uncertainty with bequest motive.

[4] Model C: medical expenses with no bequests, $F = 4{,}000$.

[5] Model D: medical expenses with bequest motive, $F = 4{,}000$.

[6] Model E: medical expenses with no bequests, $F = 2{,}000$.

[7] Model F: medical expenses with bequest motive, $F = 2{,}000$.

6.2. Comparison of Age Profiles from the HRS and the Model Simulations

To see how well the different model specifications stack up against the HRS data, we simulate our model for different assumptions about annuity-like income and household composition (marital status and longevity). For singles and married couples, we obtain separate decision rules for "high-," "medium-

," and "low-" income households, where the income categories correspond to the HRS medians for the top quintile, middle three quintiles, and the bottom quintile of retirement income—the same categories reported above. For each income group, the simulated population is chosen to match the shares of single and married households at onset of retirement in the HRS; and, for each income group, the initial level of wealth is calibrated to match the HRS data. In the simulations, individuals survive according to probabilities in the SSA age- and sex-based life-tables, so that in each period some married households become single households, and some households (mostly singles) die.

Table 10 compares median annualized wealth at different ages in the HRS (first column) with average values for annualized wealth computed from 10,000 simulated retirement periods for each of six different model specifications (denoted Model A through Model F, described in the notes to the table). The first column shows the tendency for annualized wealth to rise markedly in the HRS between households in their late 60s to their late 70s and their late 80s. The rise occurs for single and married retirees and is true whether or not economies of scale are thought to raise "effective" levels of wealth for married retirees relative to single ones.

The second column (model A) shows that, by itself, uncertain longevity cannot explain why annualized wealth rises during retirement in the HRS. Using survival rates from the SSA life tables and our assumptions for preferences and asset returns, the simulations of model A (which do not include random medical expenses or an explicit bequest motive) imply much *lower* annualized wealth for the oldest retirees (aged 85 to 90 in the table) than the youngest ones (65 to 70). This means that, for the preference specifications we have considered, precautionary motives to hold wealth against the possibility of living to very advanced ages are outweighed by the high discounting implied by low survival rates in old age.

As shown in the third column (model B), adding an explicit bequest motive to the life cycle model with uncertain longevity generates an upward-sloping age profile for annualized wealth for single retirees. Married households, however, continue to show a decline, and the simulated profile for the combined simulations (labeled "full sample") is significantly flatter than the HRS profile. In all of our simulations, singles build up more annualized wealth than married households, a pattern that can be explained by noting that individuals in the model receive a boost in annualized wealth whenever a spouse dies. The inability of model B to match the annualized wealth pattern for married couples suggests that a bequest motive is not the only factor leading retirees in the HRS to build wealth in annualized terms. For a bequest function to fit the empirical age profile of median annualized wealth, it would have to be much more powerful—in particular, retirees would have to derive more utility per dollar of wealth from their bequests than from their own consumption.

The fourth column (model C) indicates that a life cycle model with random medical expenses and a relatively high consumption floor (which reduces the precautionary incentive), but without an explicit bequest motive, gets closer to matching the upward-sloping annualized wealth profile for married households. Overall, however, the match with the full HRS sample is about the same as the model with bequests and no medical expenses. While a precautionary motive and an active bequest motive seem to induce a similar slowdown in spending, neither appears sufficiently strong to explain the data patterns by itself.

Model D shows that adding the bequest function to the model with random medical expenses and a moderate consumption floor (F = 4,000) generates a rise in annualized wealth that is quite close to the pattern for the full sample in the HRS. The bequest motive provides "extra" expected value from the precautionary buffer because accidental bequests (which will frequently arise when retirees die before having suffered a substantial random medical expense draw) convey utility value. The simulated annualized wealth levels for the three age groups ($23,400, $27,000, and $29,800) are only slightly higher than those in the data ($22,500, $26,600, and $29,000). If one were to choose a specification based only on the fit with the full sample, Model D would be the obvious selection. When we examine the results for married households, however, it is no longer clear that the model fits the best. The HRS shows a $14,000 increase in annualized wealth for married households, which is much higher than the $3,000 increase in the simulations.

Model E and model F are the same as model C and model D, but with a much lower consumption floor (F = $2, 000), which significantly strengthens the precautionary motive. This specification implies a much steeper age profile for annualized wealth for married couples, but it overshoots the annualized wealth build up for singles. For both types of households, some combination of bequests and medical expenses seems to be at work, but it is not clear which specification comes closest to the patterns in the HRS. We can learn more about the model specifications by seeing what the simulations imply about annualized wealth for the different income categories.

In terms of income heterogeneity, the main feature of the HRS data our model needs to explain is the relatively flat age profiles for the lowest income category and the very steep profiles for the highest income group. Table 11 reports the simulated and actual annualized wealth levels for households in the highest, middle three, and lowest income quintiles in the HRS. The middle rows show the same numbers as the bottom rows in Table 10, so we will focus our attention on the top and bottom income groups.

Scanning across the columns of Table 11, ones can see the importance of bequests in explaining the sharp increase in annualized wealth among higher-income households. Even with a low consumption floor, the model with medical expenses and no bequests (model E) explains much less of the increase in annualized wealth than the model with only a bequest motive (model B). Model F, which introduces the largest incentive to maintain savings in old age, comes closest to matching the patterns in the HRS for high income households, but it over-predicts the rise in annualized wealth for the middle and lower income groups. Model D, which has bequests, medical expenses, and a moderate consumption floor, misses some of the build-up in annualized wealth in the highest income category, but it comes remarkably close for the other two. It captures the flat progression of annualized wealth among lower-income households, and it almost perfectly matches the increase for the medium income group. Despite its difficulty in matching the increase in annualized wealth for married and high-income households, we conclude that a specification that includes intended bequests, uncertain medical costs, and a moderate consumption floor can account for the most prominent features of spend-down patterns in the HRS.[31]

7. Conclusion

By introducing the concept of annualized comprehensive wealth—a measure of total resources per person per expected remaining year of retirement—our analysis brings some saving patterns into relief that would otherwise be difficult to discern. Our primary empirical finding from the HRS is that annualized comprehensive wealth tends to rise with age in retirement, reflecting the tendency for wealth balances to decrease more slowly than remaining life expectancies shorten. We find this pattern of increasing annualized wealth over retirement for most types of households and for the major components of comprehensive wealth. In addition, we estimate that a much larger share of retirees experience a considerable increase in annualized comprehensive wealth over the six years covered by our HRS sample (1998 to 2004) than experience a significant decline.

Table 11. Comparison of Life-Cycle Models and Data by Income Group—Full Sample*

Age and Household Type	HRS[1]	Model A[2]	Model B[3]	Model C[4]	Model D[5]	Model E[6]	Model F[7]
Low income:							
65-70	9.00	7.65	9.28	9.36	9.36	9.62	9.63
75-80	10.50	8.76	9.48	9.70	9.74	11.42	11.52
85-90	10.00	8.53	9.05	8.95	9.12	12.23	12.57
Medium income:							
65-70	22.50	22.71	22.93	23.24	23.35	23.62	23.64
75-80	26.60	23.11	25.15	26.03	27.04	29.10	29.64
85-90	28.90	20.18	26.91	26.34	29.78	33.48	35.98
High income:							
65-70	51.50	52.09	53.04	52.99	53.33	53.20	53.46
75-80	67.60	55.37	63.08	61.01	64.93	62.86	65.49
85-90	94.90	49.81	76.01	64.53	79.34	71.55	81.71

*Annualized wealth in thousands of 2004 dollars. See text for details. The coefficient of relative risk aversion $\sigma = 3$, the bequest function is given by equation (10), and F is the value of the consumption floor.

[1]Median annualized wealth for pooled 1998-2004 sample in HRS.

[2] Model A: survival uncertainty with no bequests.

[3] Model B: survival uncertainty with bequest motive.

[4] Model C: medical expenses with no bequests, $F = 4{,}000$.

[5] Model D: medical expenses with bequest motive, $F = 4{,}000$.

[6] Model E: medical expenses with no bequests, $F = 2{,}000$.

[7] Model F: medical expenses with bequest motive, $F = 2{,}000$.

It is reasonably well known that retirees in the bottom quintile of the income distribution (conditional on their age and marital status) rely almost exclusively on DB pension benefits, Social Security benefits, and other government transfers to finance spending. Although these sources do not constitute a high level of comprehensive wealth, their annuity-like payout scheme means that they can finance a more or less constant path of outlays through retirement. While annuity-like benefits are also an important source of wealth for retirees in the middle- and upper-income groups, these retirees also tend to have significant financial and nonfinancial wealth. A new finding from our analysis is that, for the median retiree in the middle- and upper-income groups, annualized comprehensive wealth tends to rise over retirement. One might have expected wealth balances to fall roughly in line with declining longevity in retirement—after all, this is the trajectory that would be predicted by the simplest life cycle model of consumption.

To gauge what factors might lie behind the tendency for annualized comprehensive wealth to rise in retirement, we compare the empirical age profiles of annualized wealth from the HRS data with simulated profiles from life cycle models that are extended to include uncertainty about longevity, precautionary saving in light of uncertain medical expenses, and an explicit motive for retirees with greater resources to leave bequests. Within the class of models we consider, specifications that include all three of these factors seem to line up best with the rate of increase of annualized comprehensive wealth in the HRS data. In this case, saving in retirement (relative to the simplest life cycle benchmark) provides insurance against the possibility of financing consumption into advanced ages, is available to help finance possibly very large medical expenditures, and it increases the size of intended (as well as unanticipated) bequests. Quantitatively, the simulated age profiles for annualized wealth match up fairly well with the estimated profiles, although high-income households in the HRS exhibit a steeper upward trajectory for annualized wealth at older ages than the extended life cycle models predict.

REFERENCES

Aguiar, M., & Hurst E. (2005). "Consumption versus Expenditure," *Journal of Political Economy*, *113*(5), 919-48.

Anderson, K., French, E. & Lam, T. (2004). "You can't take it with you: Asset run-down at the end of the life cycle," *Economic Perspectives, Federal Reserve Bank of Chicago*, Q3, 40-54.

Attanasio, O. P., & Hoynes, H. W. (2000). "Differential Mortality and Wealth Accumulation," *Journal of Human Resources*, *35*(1), 1-29.

Benltez-Silva, H., & Dwyer D. S. (2005). "The Rationality of Retirement Expectations and the Role of New Informaton," *Review of Economics and Statistics*, *87*(3), 587-592.

________(2006). "Expectation Formation of Older Married Couples and the Rational Expectations Hypothesis," *Labour Economics, 13*, 191-218.

Bernhelm, B. D. (1987). "The Economic Effects of Social Security: Toward a Reconciliation of Theory and Measurement," *Journal of Public Economics, 33*, 273-304.

________(1991). "How Strong are Bequest Motives? Evidence Based on Estimates of the Demand for Life Insurance and Annuities," *Journal of Political Economy, 99*(5), 899-927.

________ (1992). "*Is the Baby Boom Generation Preparing Adequately for Retirement*?," Discussion paper, Merrill Lynch.

Blau, D. M. (2008). "Retirement and Consumption in a Life Cycle Model," *Journal of Labor Economics, 26*(1), 35-71.

Brown, J. R., & Poterba J. M. (2000). "Joint Life Annuities and Annuity Demand by Married Couples," *The Journal of Risk and Insurance, 67*(4), 527-553.

Cagetti, M. (2003). "Wealth Accumulation Over the Life Cycle and Precautionary Savings," *Journal of Business and Economic Statistics, 21*(3), 339-353.

Carroll, C. D. (1992). "The Buffer-Stock Theory of Saving: Some Macroeconomic Evidence," *Brookings Papers on Economic Activity, 1992*(2), 61-156.

________(1997): "Buffer-Stock Saving and the Life Cycle/Permanent Income Hypothesis," *The Quarterly Journal of Economics, 112*(1), 1-55.

Carroll, C. D., & Samwick A. A. (1998). "How Important is Precautionary Saving?," *Review of Economics and Statistics, 80*(3), 410-419.

Davies, J. B. (1981). "Uncertain Lifetime, Consumption, and Dissaving in Retirement," *The Journal of Political Economy, 89*(3), 56 1-577.

Davis, M. (2006). "*The Insurance, Health, and Savings Decisions of Elderly Women Living Alone*," Manuscript.

De Nardi, M. (2004). "Wealth Inequality and Intergenerational Links," *Review of Economic Studies, 71*, 743-768.

De Nardi, M., E. FrenCH, & Jones, J. B. (2006). "*Differential Mortality, Uncertain Medical Expenses, and the Saving of Elderly Singles*," Manuscript.

Dynan, K. E., Skinner, J. & Zeldes, S. P. (2002). "The Importance of Bequests and Life-Cycle Saving in Capital Accumulation: A New Answer," *The American Economic Review, 92*(2), 274-278.

Engen, E. M., Gale, W. G. & Uccello, C. E. (1999). "The Adequacy of Household Saving," *Brookings Papers on Economic Activity, 1999*(2), 65-187.

________ (2005). "Effects Of Stock Market Fluctuations On the Adequacy of Retirement Wealth Accumulation," *Review of Income and Wealth, 51*(3).

French, E. (2005). "The Effects of Health, Wealth, and Wages on Labor Supply and Retirement," *Review of Economic Studies, 72*, 395-427.

French, E., and Jones, J. B. (2004a). "*The Effects of Health Insurance and Self-Insurance on Retirement Behavior*," Manuscript.

________ (2004b). "On the Distribution and Dynamics of Health Care Costs," *Journal of Applied Econometrics, 19*, 705-721.

Gustman, A. L., & Steinmeler, T. L. (1998). "Effects of Pensions on Saving: Analysis with Data from the Health and Retirement Study," *NBER Working Paper No. 6681*.

Hubbard, R. G. (1987). "Uncertain Lifetimes, Pensions and Individual Saving," in *Issues in Pension Economics*, ed. by Z. Bodie, J. Shoven, and D. Wise. Chicago: NBER and the University of Chicago Press.

Hurd, M. D. (1987). "Savings of the Elderly and Desired Bequests," The *American Economic Review, 77*(3), 298-312.

(1989): "Mortality Risk and Bequests," Econometrica, 57(4), 779{813.

Hurd, M. D., & Rohwedder, S. (2006). "Some Answers to the Retirement-Consumption Puzzle," *NBER Working Paper No. 12057*, February.

Jones, D. R., Perttunen, C. D. & Stuckman, B. E. (1993). "Lipschitzian Optimization without the Lipschitz Constant," J*ournal of Optimization Theory and Applications, 79*(1), 157{181.

Kopczuk, W., & Lupton, J. P. (2007). "To Leave or Not to Leave: The Distribution of Bequest Motives," *Review of Economic Studies, 74*(1), 207-235.

Kotlikoff, L., & Summers, L. (1981). "The Role of Intergenerational Transfers in Aggregate Capital Accumulation," *Journal of Political Economy, 89*(4), 706-732.

Laitner, J., & Juster, F. T. (1996): "New Evidence on Altruism: A Study of TIAA- CREF Retirees," *The American Economic Review, 86*(4), 893-908.

Love, D. A., SMITH, & Mcnair, L. C. (2007). "Do Households Have Enough Wealth for Retirement?," *Federal Reserve Board Finance and Economics Discussion Series 2007-17*.

Mitchell, O. S., & Moore, J. F. (1998). "Can Americans Afford to Retire? New Evidence on Retirement Saving Adequacy," *Journal of Risk and Insurance, 65*(3), 371- 400.

Mitchell, O. S., POTERba, J. M. Warshawsky, M. J. & Brown, J. R. (1999). "New Evidence on the Money's Worth of Individual Annuities," *American Economic Review, 89*, 1299-1318.

Munnell, A. H., & Soto, M. (2005). "*What Replacement Rate Do Households Actually Experience in Retirement?*," Working Paper.

Munnell, A. H., Webb, A. & Delorme, L. (2006). "Retirements at Risk: A New National Retirement Index," *Boston College Center for Retirement Research*, June.

Palumbo, M. G. (1999). "Uncertain Medical Expenses and Precautionary Saving Near the End of the Life Cycle," *Review of Economic Studies, 66*(2), 395-421.

Rust, J., & Phelan, C. (1997). "How Social Security and Medicare Affect Retirement Behavior in a World of Incomplete Markets," *Econometrica, 65*(4), 781-831.

Scholz, J. K., Seshadri, A. & Khitatrakun, S. (2006). "Are Americans Saving "Optimally" For Retirement?," *Journal of Political Economy, 114*, 607-643.

Skinner, J. (2007). "Are You Sure You're Saving Enough for Retirement?," *Journal of Economic Perspectives, 21*(3), 59-80.

SSA (2006). *Period Life Table, 2002.* Social Security Administration.

Tauchen, G., & Hussey, R. (1991). "Quadrature-Based Methods for Obtaining Approximate Solutions to Nonlinear Asset Pricing Models," *Econometrica: Journal of the Econometric Society, 59*(2), 371-396.

Yaari, M. E. (1965). "Uncertain Lifetime, Life Insurance, and the Theory of the Consumer," *The Review of Economic Studies, 32*(2), 137-150.

Appendix 1: Present Value Calculations for the Annuity-Like Components of Comprehensive Wealth

In this appendix, we discuss our method for computing present values of annuitized streams of payments in the HRS. The discussion closely follows material in Love, Smith, and McNair (2007) and is repeated here for convenience.

Defined Benefit Pension Benefits

The HRS includes questions about both current pension benefits (for retirees) and expected future pension benefits (for those still working).

Households are asked about the (current or expected) pension amount (and start date, if they have not yet begun), cost-of-living adjustments (COLAs), and survivors' benefits.[32] In the case of working households, we use the expected pension at retirement; this serves to include the value of benefits not yet accrued.

We express the actuarial present value of DB payments for a plan that pays an annual amount d as

$$DBPV = d \sum_{\tau=a_r}^{119} \delta^{\tau-a_r}\{\psi^r(\tau, a_r) + \theta[1 - \psi^r(\tau, a_r)]\psi^s(\tau + \Delta, a_s)\}, \tag{A-1}$$

where δ is the discount factor, a_r and a_s are the ages of the respondent and the spouse at the time of the survey, and θ is the fraction of benefits that will be passed on to the spouse in the event that the respondent dies.[33] The term $\psi^r(\tau, a_r)$ is the probability of the respondent's living to age 'r conditional on being alive at age a_r, while $\psi^s(\tau + \Delta, a_s)$ represents the conditional survival probability of the spouse, where Δ is the age difference between the spouse and the respondent. Thus, the actuarial present value of pension wealth is just the annual pension benefit multiplied by the sum of discounted annual survival probabilities, with an extra term accounting for any payments made to the spouse after the death of the respondent.[34]

The conditional survival probabilities are based on the one-year age- and sex-specific conditional death probabilities in the Social Security Administration's 2002 Period Life Table (SSA, 2006). Period life tables provide a snapshot of the mortality conditions prevailing in a single year, rather than the expected mortality experience of a given cohort over time. For young cohorts (e.g., children born in 2002), one might expect actual longevity to be significantly greater than shown in the 2002 period life table, since longevity generally improves over time. However, since our sample is of Americans aged 51 and older in 2004, we conclude that the 2002 period table (the most recent available) is a reasonable estimate of our sample's expected mortality experience.[35]

For DB plans with COLAs (about 40 percent of the reported plans), we use a discount factor equal to $1/(1 + r)$, where r is the real interest rate. For plans without COLAs, we set equal to $1/(1+ i)$, where i is the nominal interest rate. The baseline results in the paper assume a nominal interest rate of 4.5 percent and a real interest rate of 2.5 percent, implying 2 percent inflation. The present-value measures are naturally sensitive to the value of δ. In Love,

Smith, and McNair (2007), we report results using different assumptions about real rates and inflation.

The HRS collects information on multiple pension plans for respondents and their spouses. Applying equation (A-1), we compute present values for each of these and then sum them to arrive at our final calculation for current pensions. Some current workers report that they expect to receive lump-sum payouts from their DB plans upon retirement. To include these plans, we simply discount the lump sum back to the current age:

$$DBLS = LS \sum_{\tau=a_r}^{a_r+N} \delta^{\tau-a_r} \psi^r(\tau, a_r), \tag{A-2}$$

where *LS* is the value of the lump-sum payment and *N* is the expected number of years remaining before the payout is received. We make no adjustment for survivor's benefits in the case of lump-sum payments.

Social Security Benefits

Computing the present value of of Social Security is quite similar to calculating DB wealth. The HRS includes questions about both current benefits for retirees and expected benefits for workers. Let ss_τ^r and $ss_{\tau+\Delta}^s$ $ss_{\tau+\Delta}^r$ denote the current or expected annual social security benefits of the respondent and the spouse at ages τ and $\tau + \Delta$ respectively. The actuarial present value of household Social Security benefits is given by

$$SSPV = \sum_{\tau=a_r}^{119} \delta^{\tau-a_r} \left[\Psi_1(ss_\tau^r + ss_{\tau+\Delta}^s) + \Psi_2 \max(ss_\tau^r, ss_{\tau+\Delta}^s)\right], \tag{A-3}$$

where

$$\Psi_1 = \psi^r(\tau, a_r)\psi^s(\tau + \Delta, a_s)$$

is the conditional probability of both household members being alive, and

$$\Psi_2 = \psi^r(\tau, a_r) + \psi^s(\tau + \Delta, a_s) - 2\psi^r(\tau, a_r)\psi^s(\tau + \Delta, a_s)$$

is the conditional probability of exactly one household member being alive.[36] The first bracketed term in equation (A-3) captures the fact that if both household members are alive, their total bene ts will generally equal the sum of their individual amounts. The second term in the brackets reflects the rules governing survivors benefits, whereby a retirement-age widow or widower typically receives 100% of the spouse's bene ts if these exceed their own bene t amount.[37] Since Social Security bene ts are adjusted for in ation, we discount using the real interest rate: $\delta = 1 = (1 + r)$.

Respondents in the HRS are asked directly about the amount of current or expected spousal benefits. We take these amount at face value and assume that the reported benefits already reflect any adjustments due to the Social Security rules (e.g., the fact that individuals are typically entitled to the maximum of their own benefits and 50% of their spouse's).[38]

Annuities and Welfare Benefits

Our calculations of wealth from annuities and welfare payments are more straightforward. The formula for calculating the actuarial present value of annuities (*ANPV*) exactly parallels equation (A-1), where we make similar adjustments for COLAs and survivor benefits. Our measure of expected welfare payments includes veteran's benefits, food stamps, Supplemental Security Income (SSI), and other welfare. In this calculation, we assume that individuals who are currently receiving these payments will continue to receive the same inflation-indexed welfare payments as long as they live, and that those not currently receiving these payments never will—i.e., we do not model transitions in and out of welfare-receipt status. Since welfare benefits are typically indexed to inflation, we discount this stream of expected welfare payments using the real interest rate and the relevant conditional survival probabilities.

APPENDIX 2: DETAILED DESCRIPTION OF THE LIFE CYCLE MODEL SIMULATIONS REPORTED IN THE PAPER

Simulation Results

The solution to the model consists of a set of decision rules for consumption that depend on current assets, age, and in the case of medical expenses, the value of the current shock. With these decision rules in hand, we simulate various life histories, making different assumptions about initial assets. Where there is any uncertainty, we conduct 10,000 Monte Carlo simulations and present the resulting average profiles of consumption, financial assets, and annualized wealth. We simulate four main variations of the life-cycle model described above: (1) a baseline model with no survival uncertainty or medical expenses; (2) a model with only uncertain survival; (3) a model with uncertain survival and medical expenses; and (4) models (1) through (3) with an operative bequest motive.

Baseline Life Cycle Model

Panel (a) in Figure A-1 shows the simulation results for the baseline life cycle model specification, in which all retirees know they will live exactly to their life expectancy, do not face random medical expense shocks, and do not value leaving bequests. One thing that stands out in that panel is the abrupt decline in income at age 82. The decline, smoother versions of which we will see in all of our simulations, is due to the fact that households receive less Social Security income when one of the members dies. Apart from income, the figure reproduces the familiar results of the standard life-cycle model. Wealth declines steadily through retirement, and consumption lies almost entirely on top of annualized wealth at all ages. This is a reflection of the central hypothesis of thc standard life-cycle model: in the absence of bequests or income uncertainty, households will optimally consume their permanent income, which in this case is exactly equal to annualized wealth. In order to explain the upward-sloping annualized wealth profiles observed in the data, we will have to consider departures from the baseline model. We begin by considering the role of uncertain longevity.

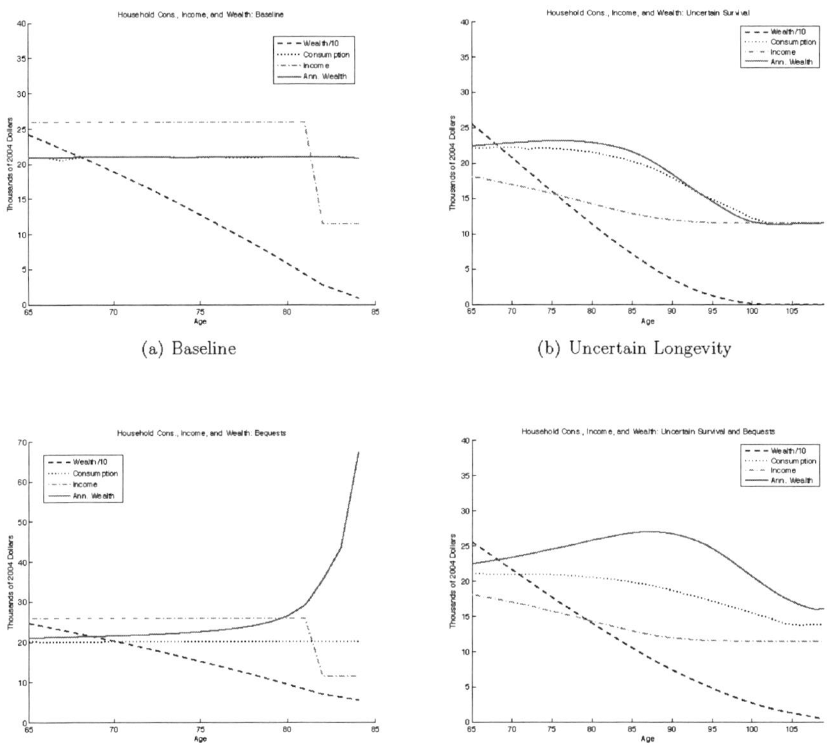

(a) Baseline

(b) Uncertain Longevity

(c) Bequest Function with Certain Longevity

(d) Bequest Function with Uncertain Longevity

Figure A-1. Effect of Uncertain Longevity and a Bequest Function on Consumption and Annualized Wealth

Effect of Uncertain Longevity

Panel (b) displays average life-cycle profiles for households facing uncertain longevity. Annualized wealth and consumption now rise gradually until almost age 80 and then fall rapidly until they equal retirement income around age 95. From the value function in equation (7), we can see that survival probabilities act like the discount factor to depress the growth rate of consumption. Individuals recognize that they may not live to enjoy future consumption, so they spend more today. This discounting effect accounts for the rapid spend-down past age 80, but what, then, explains the upward sloping profiles earlier in retirement?

The increase in average consumption and annualized wealth is due to the fact that some spouses die earlier than anticipated. Early in retirement, households prepare to finance consumption for both members over their expected lifespans. Some households will live longer than expected and risk exhausting their resources. Others will experience an early death, and the surviving spouses will find themselves with a sudden increase in total resources per person, which translates into an increase in both annualized wealth and consumption. The upward-sloping portion in panel (b) reflects the tendency for this "surviving spouse" effect to dominate the discounting effect of uncertain survival. When we model only single-headed households, there is no "surviving spouse" effect, and the average profiles for consumption and annualized wealth fall throughout retirement. Even with joint households, however, the increase in annualized wealth is not nearly strong enough to match the rise in the data. We can get closer to the upward-sloping profile in the HRS data by introducing a bequest function to the model.

Effect of a Bequest Function

An important deviation from this simple model, and one that has received a great deal of attention in the literature, is the inclusion of an explicit bequest motive. If individuals intend to bequeath wealth to their heirs, they will naturally maintain a larger stock of financial wealth than those without a bequest motive. As these individual progress through retirement, the annualized value of this wealth will continue to rise until it reaches the value of bequests in the last period of life. To see whether bequests have the potential to explain the annualized wealth patterns in the data, we solved a life-cycle model assuming that households value bequests according to the function given by equation (10).

Adding a bequest function to the model moves us a step closer to the rising annualized wealth profiles in the data, but not all the way. Panels (c) and (d) show annualized wealth profiles for the cases of certain uncertain survival. Bequests tilt up the annualized wealth in both cases, with a marked increase toward the end of life. In the certain survival case, the sharp increase is due to the fact that the amount of wealth targeted for bequests remains constant, while the remainder of resources declines to finance consumption. When financial wealth is large, bequests have only a small effect on annualized wealth, but toward the end of life, the bequest becomes large relative to consumption needs, and annualized wealth blows up.

Effect of Differential Mortality by Wealth

De Nardi, French, and Jones (2006) estimate a life-cycle model populated by elderly singles and find that differential mortality (by gender, health, and earnings) plays a significant role in explaining the low rates of dissaving among the highest permanent income households. They find, for example, that median assets for individuals in the top income quintile would fall by $10,000 if they had the same survival probabilities as healthy males in the middle of the income distribution. To get a sense for whether differential mortality is likely to exert a strong enough influence on consumption behavior to explain the data, we run a simple experiment that focuses only on single males. We solve life-cycle model with three different sets of survival probabilities: a medium one that replicates the SSA life tables, a high one that one that multiplies survival rates by 1.2, and a low one that multiplies the survival rates in the life tables by 0.8.

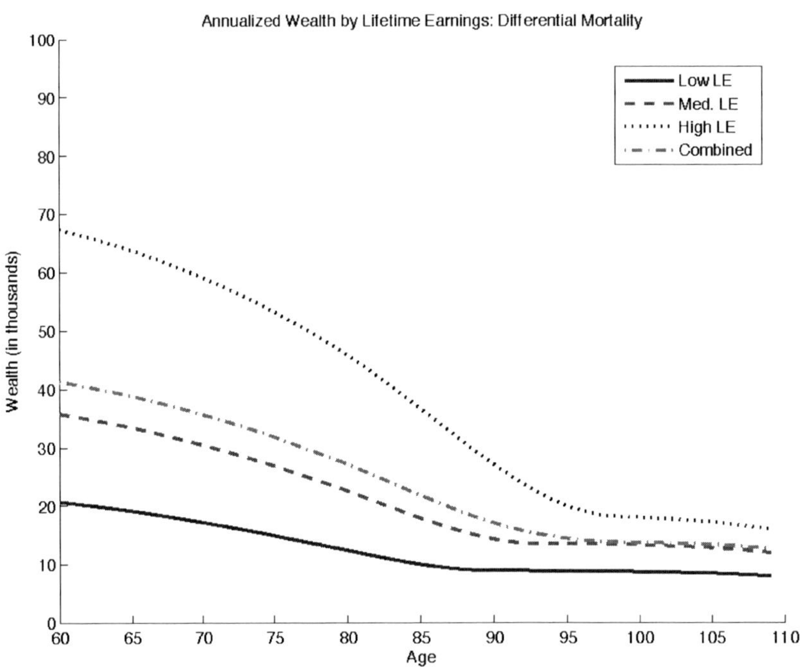

Figure A-2. The Effect of Differential Mortality by Wealth on the Age Profile of Annualized Wealth

Figure A-2 shows how the differential-mortality adjusted annualized wealth path (labeled "combined") differs from the unadjusted profiles for each of the mortality groups. We constructed the experiment so that the average value of initial wealth for all three groups is exactly equal to the initial wealth for just the medium mortality group. The medium mortality group therefore provides a baseline for the combined profile. From the figure, it appears unlikely that the magnitude of the difference between the low and high case is sufficient to explain the strongly upward sloping trend of annualized wealth observed in the data. The combined profile lies above the medium profile, but only by a slight amount, and not nearly enough to suggest a promising role for differential mortality to explain the empirical profiles. Our simulation results are not inconsistent with the findings in De Nardi, French, and Jones (2006), as we also find that longer-lived households dissave more gradually. It is just that the effect of differential mortality alone does not appear strong enough to explain the upward-sloping annualized wealth profiles we observe in the data.

Effect of Random Medical Expenses

Older individuals face increasing risks of poor health and large out-of-pocket medical expenses. Because Medicare provides only limited coverage for long-term care, a string of adverse health shocks can potentially wipe out a household's financial assets. At the same time, changes in health status can also alter an individual's enjoyment of consumption and leisure. Given that the incidence and severity of health shocks tends to rise with age, health may provide a key to understanding the upward sloping path of annualized wealth.

Figure A-3 displays the life-cycle profiles both with and without bequests. The left panels correspond to the specification with a high consumption floor ($4,000) and the right panels to the low floor ($2,000).[39] The figures indicate that households accrue significantly more annualized resources as a precaution against out-of-pocket medical expenses that can potentially wipe out retirement wealth. Not surprisingly, the utility consequences of high medical costs depend on the size of the consumption floor. Regardless of the existence of a bequest motive, reducing the size of the consumption floor has a substantial effect on the build-up of annualized wealth.

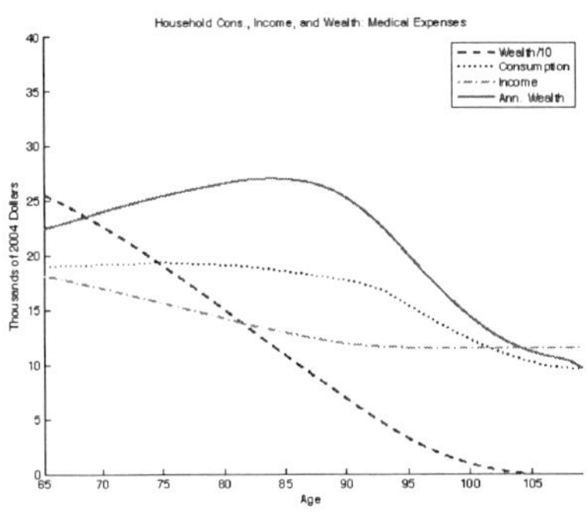

(a) Medical Costs with High Floor ($F = 4,000$)

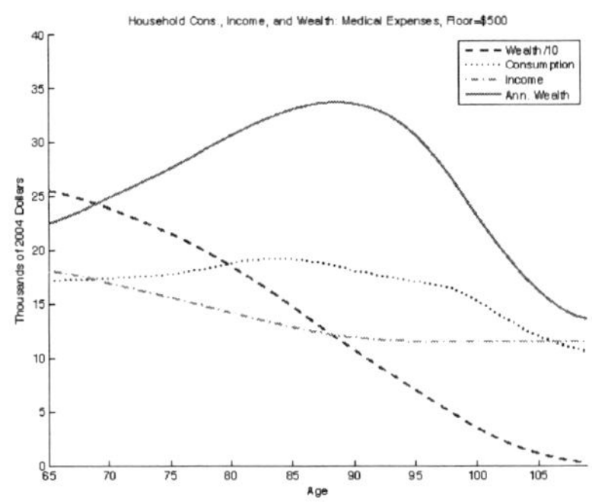

(b) Medical Costs with Low Floor ($F = 2,000$)

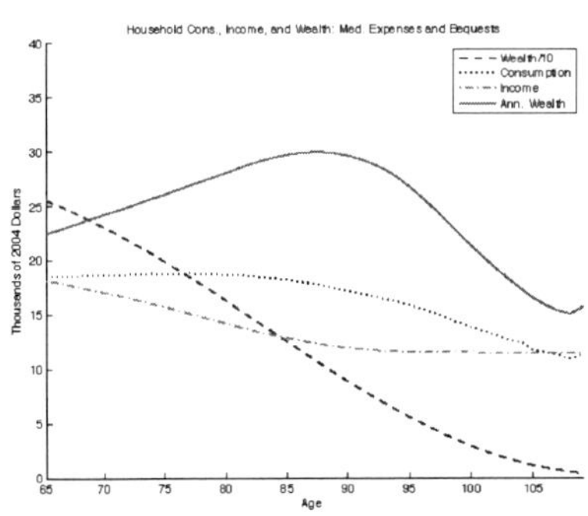

(c) Medical Costs and a Bequest Function with High Floor ($F = 4,000$)

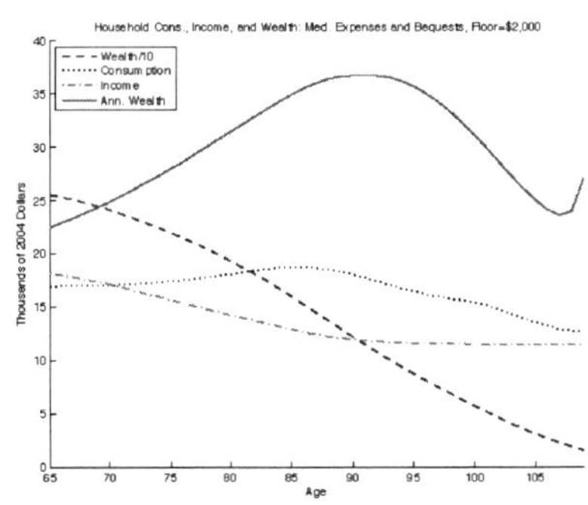

(d) Medical Costs and a Bequest Function with Low Floor ($F = 2,000$)

Figure A-3. Effect of Random Medical Expenses and a Bequest Function on Consumption and Annualized Wealth

End Notes

* This research was conducted (in part) with the support of the 2007 Sandell Grant for Retirement Research, sponsored by the Center for Retirement Research at Boston College. We have benefited from helpful comments from Hugo Ben´ıtez-Silva, Marco Cagetti, Chris Carroll, Karen Dynan, Eric French, Erik Hurst, Howard Iams, David Laibson, Annamaria Lusardi, John Sabelhaus, Jonathan Skinner, and seminar participants at the Federal Reserve Board, ASSA Annual Meeting, SUNY Stony Brook, and the City University of New York. In addition, we thank Lucy McNair for outstanding research assistance. The views expressed herein are those of the authors and do not necessarily reflect those of the Board of Governors or the staff of the Federal Reserve System

1 Although annualized wealth will track consumption in certain specifications of a life-cycle model, the two will generally differ. It should not, therefore, be interpreted as a measure of welfare.

[2] See Skinner (2007) for a recent perspective on the literature.

[3] In related work looking at the rationality of expectations about retirement, Benitez-Silva and Dwyer (2005, 2006) find that older households appear to form expectations in a way that is consistent with rational behavior.

[4] We could extend the panel further back for some, but not all, cohorts, since 1998 was the first wave to represent the full age distribution of older households. In the text, we frequently refer to households in our sample as "retirees" even though some report to the HRS that they are still working outside the home.

[5] Survivorship bias arises from the tendency of lower-wealth households to die younger than higher-wealth households, distorting the observed time path of median wealth in the data. We use the balanced "2004- backward" panel for tabulations presented in the paper, but we use the larger unbalanced "1998-forward" panel for estimating our regression-based age profiles, because survivorship bias is less of an issue when looking directly at household-level changes between adjacent waves of the survey (just two years apart).

[6] The actuarial present value calculation discounts expected future streams of income by the probability of death as well as a time discount factor, taking into account any survivor's benefits. See Appendix 1 for details.

[7] Nonetheless, as we will see, annuity-like wealth can fall even relative to life expectancy, because DB pensions may not be fully inflation-indexed.

[8] Note that net housing wealth can be affected by three different forces: purchases or sales of assets (including "downsizing" to smaller homes or changing tenure from homeowner to renter), changes in borrowing (including mortgage pay-offs or new equity extraction via cash-out refinancings or reverse mortgages), and capital gains on owned homes.

[9] If no spouse is present, we set $T_t^m = 0$, , and the expression collapses to $a_t = \frac{r}{1+r}\left[1 - \frac{1}{(1+r)^{T_t^f}}\right]^{-1}$.

[10] The factor $1+r$ in the denominator reflects the fact that we are not discounting the first period's interest.

[11] Prices for actual fixed life annuities in the U.S. are far from actuarially fair; for example, see Mitchell, Poterba, Warshawsky, and Brown (1999).

'[12] In our formulation, we assume that the annuity payments begin immediately, so that the first payment is not discounted.

'[13] For practical purposes, Social Security is such an annuity. Thus, annualized wealth is like the sum of Social Security benefits and an actuarially fair, inflation-indexed annuity that could (in principle) be purchased with the value of all other net assets.

[14] We begin with nonparametric age profiles to get a sense of the raw data patterns before imposing any structural assumptions.

[15] Thus, for this exercise we use the unbalanced 1998-forward panel, rather than the balanced 2004- backward panel. We use the HRS sampling weights to compute the medians in each age group.

[16] For example, younger cohorts may be wealthier because they earned higher lifetime wages, due to productivity growth.

[17] As reported in tables 4 and 7, we define "high" income as the top quintile of household income, "medium" income as the middle three quintiles, and "low" income as the bottom quintile. To control for cohort and demographic differences, we calculate quintiles conditional on age and marital status (so that, for example, the "high-income" group is not disproportionately composed of young married households).

[18] We use two-year age bins, rather than single-year age indicators, simply to smooth the age profiles a bit. The results are qualitatively similar when we use single-year age dummies.

[19] For example, if the predicted median growth factor for age 60-61 were 1.10 and the predicted median growth factor for age 62-63 were 1.05, then the predicted cumulative growth factor for age 62-63 would be 1.10 * 1.05 = 1.155.

[20] Note that since these lines are fitted values from median regressions, the line for comprehensive wealth does not equal the sum of the lines for the three major components of wealth.

[21] As noted above, real annualized DB wealth may fall in retirement because benefits are usually not indexed to inflation.

[22] For example, the change in the Wilshire 5000 stock price index between 1998 and 2000 was 7.6 percent, between 2000 and 2002 was -31.5 percent, and between 2002 and 2004 was 43.5 percent.

[23] For example, on a seasonally adjusted basis, the change in the national purchase-only house price index produced by the Office of Federal Housing Enterprise Oversight (OFHEO) between 1998 and 2000 was 13.8 percent, between 2000 and 2002 was 16.1 percent, and between 2002 and 2004 was 19.4 percent.

[24] We also looked at similarly-constructed counterfactual nonparametric age profiles (not shown) and found that, looking across cohorts in the HRS, older households had more housing wealth, relative to life expectancy, than did younger households, even before the changes in market prices from 1998 to 2004.

[25] The appendix includes a more thorough discussion of how uncertain longevity, random medical expenses, and the bequest function affect optimal consumption and annualized wealth in our life-cycle models.

[26] See, for example, Cagetti (2003); Carroll (1992, 1997) and Carroll and Samwick (1998) for models of precautionary saving in response to uncertain income, Palumbo (1999); Rust and Phelan (1997); French and Jones (2004a); Anderson, French, and Lam (2004) and Davis (2006) for studies of the effect of uncertain medical expenses, and Kotlikoff and Summers (1981); Hurd (1987, 1989); Bernheim (1991); Laitner and Juster (1996); Dynan, Skinner, and Zeldes (2002); De Nardi (2004) and Kopczuk and Lupton (2007) for models incorporating explicit bequest motives.

[27] A complete treatment of the life cycle from the beginning of working life would introduce potentially interesting sources of heterogeneity in wealth and retirement income, but this type of heterogeneity is not the focus of our analysis. For our purposes, little is lost by starting our model at retirement, and we gain transparency and simplicity since we can show how different factors affect consumption patterns independent of *initial retirement wealth*.

[28] We have solved the model for other values of risk aversion, but we obtained a good fit using $\sigma = 3$.

[29] With $\sigma = 3$, if we were to set $b_1 = 1$, there would be very little incentive in the model for households to leave sizable bequests. Note that our bequest specification nests most of the bequest functions used in previous studies (see, e.g., De Nardi (2004) for a careful study of bequest functions). We experimented with several different values for the parameters b_1 and b_2, and found similar results across the various simulations.

[30] The consumption floor introduces nonconvexities into the value function that rule out gradient-based optimization techniques. We use a global optimization algorithm called DIRECT, or DIviding RECTangles (Jones, Perttunen, and Stuckman, 1993).

[31] Note that it is difficult to completely disentangle the effects of intentional bequests from higher-income retirees planning to spend significantly more on medical care when they are very old.

[32] We are using self-reported pension data to calculate pension wealth. Restricted versions of the HRS also include employer-provided pension data that in some cases may provide a more accurate measure of pension benefits (see Gustman and Steinmeier (1998)). The main differences between the self-reported measures that we use and the supplemental data involve workers' **expectations of future pensions**. Because most of our sample consists of retirees who are currently receiving pensions, we expect our results to be robust to our reliance on the self-reported data for workers.

[33] We ignore non-spouse beneficiaries. If there is no spouse, we set θ to zero.

[34] Bernheim (1987) argues that actuarial discounting is inappropriate for risk-averse individuals facing imperfect annuity markets, because such individuals would attach additional value to the otherwise unavailable insurance product. He suggests straight discounting (ignoring the probability of death) instead. However, he points out that his analysis rests on the premise that individuals place no value on the death-contingent value of assets (i.e., that there are no bequest motives). We treat the household as a unit, and explicitly value the death-contingent component of each individual's assets (e.g., survivors' benefits and life insurance). Thus we use the actuarial present value of DB and Social Security benefits. Note that we are only computing the amount of wealth, and not the utility value of that wealth. Similarly, we make no adjustment in the PV calculation for the utility value of risk (e.g., longevity risk or the risk of a large medical-expense shock.)

[35] Note that these are average survival for the population. Thus, to the extent that, for example, lower- wealth respondents face lower survival probabilities than higher-wealth respondents, our calculations will tend to overstate the pension wealth of the lower-wealth groups and to understate the pension wealth of the higher-wealth groups. In future work we hope to use wealth-adjusted survival probabilities to test the effect of differential mortality on our results. However, we would not expect this to be too much of a problem because differential mortality seems to be evident primarily at very old ages (see Anderson, French, and Lam (2004) and Attanasio and Hoynes (2000)), where heavy discounting is already being applied for most retirees.

[36] To see the intuition of this expression, note that the equation for $\Psi 2$ is simply a rearrangement of $\psi^r(1-\psi^s)+\psi^s(1-\psi^r)$.

[37] Widows older than 60 but younger than the full retirement age generally receive 70 percent of the workers' benefit.

[38] Restricted versions of the HRS also include Social Security earnings records for a majority of respondents, from which, with sufficient care, more accurate calculations of future Social Security benefits can be calculated. In future work we hope to use these records, though we would not expect these data to make a lot of difference for our calculations because most of our sample is already receiving benefits.

[39] The simulations assume that households begin retirement in one of the two lowest medical expense states, after which point medical expenses follow the stochastic process in the model.

In: Financial Asset Management and Wealth... ISBN: 978-1-60741-696-8
Editor: Terrance G. Waverly

Chapter 2

CONVERTING RETIREMENT SAVINGS INTO INCOME: ANNUITIES AND PERIODIC WITHDRAWALS*

Janemarie Mulvey[1] and Patrick Purcell[2]

SUMMARY

To a worker contemplating retirement, there is perhaps no more important question than "How long will my money last?" Congress has a strong interest in the income security of older Americans because much of their income is either provided directly from public programs like Social Security, or in the case of pensions and retirement accounts, is subsidized through tax deductions and deferrals.

Many retirees must decide how to convert retirement account balances into income and how to preserve the accounts in the face of several kinds of risk.

- *Longevity risk* is the risk that the individual will exhaust his or her account before death and experience a substantial decline in income.

* This is an edited, reformatted and augmented version of a CRS Report for Congress publication dated February 2009.

- *Investment risk* is the risk that the assets in which the individual has invested his or her retirement account will decline in value.
- *Inflation risk* is the risk that price increases will cause the individual's retirement income to decline in purchasing power.
- *Unexpected events* such as divorce, the death of a spouse, the cost of medical care, or a need for long-term care services are also risks.

There are strategies for dealing with each of these risks, but no single strategy can deal effectively with all of them. For example, purchasing a life annuity insures against longevity risk and it shifts the investment risk to the insurer. However, purchasing an annuity depletes the purchaser's available assets by the amount of the premium. These assets are no longer available to the retiree in the event of a catastrophic illness or other unexpected major expense. To date, the demand for annuities has been low. There are many reasons for the low demand for annuities, but one of the most important has been that many potential annuity purchasers do not value the longevity insurance provided by annuities at its market price.

Retirees who choose not to purchase life annuities must decide how much to withdraw from their retirement accounts each year. Because they face uncertainty with respect to both life expectancy and the rate of return on investment, this decision carries its own risks. If withdrawals are too large, retirees risk spending down their savings too quickly, possibly leaving them impoverished. If withdrawals are too small, they might spend too little and leave substantial assets unspent when they die.

An analysis conducted by CRS indicates that under specific conditions there is a 95% or greater probability that a man who retires at age 65 will not exhaust his retirement account before the earlier of death or age 95 if his initial withdrawal does not exceed 5% of the account balance and later withdrawals are the same in inflation-adjusted dollars. Under the same conditions, there is a 95% or greater probability that a woman who retires at age 65 will not exhaust her retirement account before the earlier of death or age 95 if her initial withdrawal does not exceed 4.5% of the account balance and later withdrawals are the same in inflation-adjusted dollars.

INTRODUCTION

The 78 million members of the "baby boom" generation are beginning to retire.[1] After many years of accumulating assets to spend in retirement, they now must decide how to convert these assets into a steady stream of income. Because of the trend away from defined benefit (DB) pensions to defined contribution (DC) plans—such as 401(k) plans—future retirees will be less likely to have a guaranteed stream of income from defined benefit pensions. Furthermore, while Social Security will provide a guaranteed income to most retirees, it will replace only a relatively small proportion of their pre-retirement income.[2] As a result of these trends, many future retirees will rely greatly on their savings to finance their consumption during retirement.

A retiree who is deciding how to convert wealth into retirement income will have to balance many risks. Increases in average life expectancy will mean that future retirees will have to ensure that their wealth will last through a retirement that could span 30 or 40 years. Increased volatility in equity markets, the effects of inflation on purchasing power, and the possibility of substantial expenses for medical treatment and long-term care will further complicate this decision.

There are a number of ways to convert retirement wealth into income. One option is to purchase a life annuity from an insurance company. In exchange for payment of an initial premium, a life annuity pays a guaranteed income throughout retirement, regardless of how long the purchaser lives.[3] Life annuities represent only about 5% of individual annuities sold in the United States. Most annuities sold in the U.S. are deferred annuities, which are tax-deferred retirement savings accounts. At retirement, a deferred annuity can be converted to a life annuity; yet, relatively few deferred annuities are converted to life annuities. Likewise, most individuals who have accumulated retirement savings in 401(k) plans or individual retirement accounts (IRAs) choose to access these funds through lump-sum distributions or periodic withdrawals rather than by purchasing a life annuity.

There are many reasons why relatively few retirees choose to purchase a life annuity as a source of retirement income.[4] Among these reasons are that

- most retirees receive annuity income from Social Security;
- about one-third of retirees receive annuity income from defined benefit pensions;
- the fees charged by annuity providers can be high and the fee structure is not transparent;

- purchasing an annuity reduces the assets available to the retiree to meet unexpected expenses, and breaking the contract is costly; and
- there have been instances of deceptive sales practices by some agents, many of whom receive large commissions for each sale.

Another option for converting retirement savings into income is to take periodic withdrawals from a retirement account. Some retirees attempt to "self-annuitize" by basing the amount of each periodic withdrawal from the account on their remaining life expectancies. Retirees who selfannuitize take on the responsibility of managing their investments and also the risk that they will live longer than average.

This report has two sections. The first section describes four kinds of risk that retirees face in retirement: longevity risk, investment risk, inflation risk, and the risk of large, unexpected expenses for medical care or long-term care. It then describes the basic features of life annuities and examines some of the reasons that the market for these annuities remains small, in spite of the protection that they provide against outliving one's retirement assets. The second section of the report describes various strategies for self-annuitizing and presents the results of an analysis that CRS conducted to estimate the probability that an individual who elects to self-annuitize would exhaust his or her retirement assets before death.

THE NATURE OF RISK IN RETIREMENT

Decisions about how to draw down assets in retirement must take into account many risks. These include longevity risk (i.e., the risk that one will live beyond the average life expectancy), inflation risk, investment risk, and the risk associated with unexpected financial shocks from widowhood, divorce, medical care, or the need for long-term care services.

Longevity Risk

The U.S. population is living longer than previous generations. A man who reached age 65 in 1960 could expect to live another 13.0 years, while a woman who turned 65 in 1960 had a remaining life expectancy of 15.8 years. A man who reached age 65 in 2004 could expect to live another 17.1 years, while a woman who turned 65 in 2004 had a remaining life expectancy of 20.0

years.[5] Looking beyond the averages, more than one-fourth of women who reach age 65 are likely to live to age 90, and 12.4% are likely to live to age 95. One out of six men who attain age 65 will live to age 90, and an estimated 6% will live to age 95. (See **Table 1**). Individuals who underestimate the likelihood of living into very old age might spend their assets too quickly, depleting their savings while they still have many years to live. This could lead to a decline in their standard of living, and possibly to increased reliance on public assistance programs.

Table 1. Estimated Percentage of Individuals Age 65 in 2004 Surviving to Selected Ages

Surviving to Age	Total	Male	Female
75	66.6	60.3	72.7
80	53.9	46.5	61.0
85	38.3	30.6	45.4
90	22.2	15.9	27.8
95	9.4	5.8	12.4
100	2.5	1.3	3.5

Source: U.S. National Center for Health Statistics, National Vital Statistics Report, *United States Life Tables, 2004*, vol. 56(9), (December 2007).

Inflation Risk

As overall prices in the economy rise over time, the purchasing power of income declines unless income increases at the same rate that prices increase. Few pensions in the private sector provide regular cost-of-living increases. Data collected by the Department of Labor indicate that fewer than 5% of pensions in the private sector provide regular cost-of-living adjustments to retirees. Retirees must account for the potential impact of inflation on their investment portfolios as they decide how to draw down their retirement wealth.

Social Security is one of the few sources of retirement income that is fully inflation-indexed each year. Yet, even Social Security's annual cost-of-living adjustments may not fully protect retirement income from the effects of inflation. The annual cost-of-living adjustment for Social Security is based on the increase in the overall level of prices. Prices for some categories of expenditures that the elderly use at higher rates than younger consumers –

such as health care – have been growing faster than overall prices. Over the period from 1980 to 2007, the average annual rate of inflation for goods and services averaged 3.5%, but prices for medical care rose at an average annual rate of 5.9%.[6] For those who have above-average out-of-pocket health care expenditures, these price increases can significantly reduce the amount of income available for other expenditures. In addition, Medicare Part B premium increases are tied to program cost increases which have historically exceeded growth in general inflation.[7] By 2025, these premiums are expected to equal over 50% of the average Social Security benefit, as compared to 27% in 2006.[8]

Investment Risk

Investment risk is the possibility that an individual's retirement assets might decline in value because specific stocks, bonds, or other assets depreciate. Diversification can reduce investment risk, because declines in the value of some assets are likely to be fully or partially offset by gains in the value of other assets. Stock and bond mutual funds, for example, help protect individuals from investment risk by purchasing securities from many companies in a variety of industries. In a mutual fund, investment losses from companies that are performing poorly may be offset by investment gains from companies that are performing well.

Investment risk includes market risk, which is the possibility that an individual's retirement assets will decline in value because of an overall decline in asset prices, as when the stock market falls. Even a well-diversified portfolio of stocks will not protect the value of an individual's retirement from depreciating if stock values fall across the board, as they have in 2008. Although a diversified portfolio can moderate investment risk, there have been extended periods of time when declines in the stock market and low interest rates resulted in negative returns on investment. For example, between 1929 to 2006 there were 14 ten-year periods of negative annual rates of return after adjusting for inflation. **Table 2** shows the five worst of those 14 ten- year periods. There have also been instances when negative rates of return spanned 15 years. Between 1966 and 1981, real rates of return on stocks averaged -0.4%, and the average annual real rate of return on short-term government securities was -0.2%.[9] Those who retire at the beginning of a period of negative returns could face significant reductions in retirement wealth.

Unexpected Events

Unexpected events can adversely affect retirement income. These include losing a spouse through death or divorce, high medical expenses, and the need for long-term care services. According to a recent study by the Urban Institute, more than two-thirds of adults age 70 and older experienced at least one such financial shock over a nine-year period. Widowhood occurred among nearly one-third of married adults over age 70. The study found that widowhood was more likely to reduce women's wealth than men's wealth.[10]

Unexpected health care costs can also reduce retirement wealth. Although the majority of retirees are covered by Medicare, deductibles and co-payments can be significant for those who are seriously ill. Medicare provides only limited coverage for long-term hospital stays and nursing home care. A recent analysis of the Health and Retirement Survey found that 6% of households aged 75-84 paid more than 50% of their income for out-of-pocket medical expenses.[11] These costs can be especially high at the end of life when a surviving spouse may face large medical bills and an accompanying reduction in retirement income. A study in 2002 found that out-of- pocket costs for end-of-life medical expenses could average about $23,000 (adjusted to 2007 dollars).[12] While the introduction of Medicare Part D may offset some of these costs, even under this program an individual who is not eligible for a low-income subsidy could be responsible for more than $6,000 in copayments for prescription medicines in 2009.

Another potential economic shock is the cost of long-term care services.[13] It has been estimated that over two-thirds of individuals aged 65 and older will require long-term care services at some point in their lives. In 2008, the annual average cost of a nursing home stay is $68,255 for a semiprivate room and $76,285 for a private room.[14] These costs greatly exceed the 2007 median income of $29,730 among households in which either the householder or householder's spouse was 65 or older.[15] Medicare does not cover extended stays in nursing homes, and Medicaid coverage generally is available only to individuals who are poor or become poor by spending down their assets on long-term care services.[16] For those who are not Medicaid-eligible and who have not purchased private long-term care insurance, long-term care costs must be paid out-of- pocket.

ANNUITIES AS A SOURCE OF RETIREMENT INCOME

A life annuity – also called an immediate annuity – is an insurance contract that provides income payments on specified dates in return for an initial premium. Life annuities can help protect retirees against some of the financial risks of retirement, especially longevity risk and investment risk. Life annuities pay income to the purchaser for as long as he or she lives, and in the case of joint-and survivor annuities, for as long as the surviving spouse lives. In addition, some annuities offer limited protection against inflation through annual increases. However, the annual increases must be paid for by accepting a lower initial monthly annuity income. Other annuities allow the purchaser to share in the investment gains from growth in equity markets as a way to offset the effects of inflation; however, such annuities also require the purchaser to share in the investment losses if markets fall.

Despite the potential advantages of annuities in reducing longevity risk and investment risk, life annuities continue to represent a small proportion of all annuities sold in the U.S. In recent years, deferred annuities – used as tax-deferred savings vehicles – have outsold life annuities by a ratio of almost 20 to 1.[17] As noted earlier, the irrevocable nature of annuity contracts appears to be an important factor in dissuading many retirees from purchasing life annuities. Although insurers have devised options to assure that the payments will continue after the purchaser's death – jointand-survivor annuities, and term-certain annuities, for example – these options add to the cost of the annuity. Because of the projected increase in the number of older Americans over the next 20 years, and the concurrent increase in the potential market for life annuities, insurers are likely to continue to add features to their annuity products in an attempt to broaden their appeal to retirees.

Table 2. Annual Average Rate of Return Over 10-Year Period (adjusted for inflation)

	Portfolio Mix	
Time Period	**65% Stocks/35% Bonds**	**65% Bonds/35% Stocks**
1968 to 1978	-4.3	-1.8
1972 to 1982	-4.0	-1.7
1964 to 1974	-3.9	-1.3
1971 to 1981	-3.8	-1.6
1938 to 1948	-3.6	-3.4

Source: CRS analysis of data from Ibottson Associates.

The Current Market for Annuities

Annuities are either provided through employer-sponsored pension plans (the group market) or are purchased directly by individuals (the individual market).

Group Annuities

Annuities from defined-benefit pensions can protect retirees from investment risk and longevity risk. The benefit formula under most defined benefit pensions is based on the worker's years of service and final average salary. The individual's benefit does not vary with investment returns, nor does it decrease as a result of increases in average life-expectancy.[18] The employer that sponsors the plan bears both the investment risk and the longevity risk. If investment returns fall below expectations, or if the plan's actuaries project increases in life expectancy, the plan sponsor must provide additional funding to the plan to meet these costs. Since the mid-1980s, the proportion of workers who retire with a defined benefit pension has declined substantially. The number of workers participating in defined benefit pension plans fell from 26.9 million in 1985 to 20.6 million in 2006, a decline of 23%.[19]

Another reason for the decline in the number of workers retiring with an employer-sponsored annuity has been an increase in the number of defined benefit plans that offer the option of taking a lump-sum rather than an annuity. Of all those who are covered under a defined benefit plan, more than half are offered the choice between a lump sum and an annuity.[20] When offered this choice, many individuals choose the lump-sum option. According to a study by the Vanguard Group, only 40% of defined benefit plan participants who are offered a lump-sum choose to receive an annuity.[21] Given these trends, the share of retirement income that will be guaranteed in the form of a defined benefit annuity is likely to decline in the future.

Individual Annuities

Annuities purchased directly from insurance companies or from insurance agents or brokers by individuals are called individual annuities. Two features that vary across individual annuities are the timing of payments and the rates of return.

Timing of Payments

Annuities can either be *deferred*, in that premiums are paid and assets are accumulated while the individual is working and payment of income is deferred until the worker retires, or *immediate*, in which a single premium is paid in exchange for lifelong stream of income that begins immediately.

A deferred annuity is similar to a savings account in which individuals can accumulate money over time. Investment earnings accrue on a tax-deferred basis. Deferred annuities represent nearly 95 percent of annuity sales. While individuals holding a deferred annuity can convert the funds into a guaranteed stream of income in retirement, most take a lump-sum payment or a series of periodic withdrawals.[22]

An immediate annuity provides a guaranteed monthly income for a specified period of time in exchange for a one-time premium payment. Income from an annuity can be either fixed or variable. Income from an annuity may be a received for specific number of years, as with a *term certain annuity*, for the life of the annuitant, as in a *single-life annuity*, or for the lives of both the annuitant and his or her spouse, as in a *joint and survivor annuity*. Under a joint and survivor annuity, the surviving spouse is eligible to receive income until he or she dies. The survivor benefit is typically 50%, 75%, or 100% of the income received while the annuity purchaser was living. As noted earlier, while immediate annuities can protect retirees from longevity risk and transfer the investment risk to the insurer, only 5% of individual annuities currently sold are immediate annuities.[23]

Table 3 shows some examples of monthly income from an immediate annuity. Most annuities purchased in the private sector provide different incomes for men and women. Men can purchase an annuity with a higher monthly income than women for the same premium because the average life expectancy of a man is lower than for a woman of the same age. The average lifetime values of the annuities for a man and woman of the same age would be equal. Employer-sponsored pension plans must offer unisex annuities to retirees.[24] Under a unisex annuity, a man would receive a lower monthly annuity income than he would get from a gender-based annuity, reflecting the higher average life expectancy of a group that includes both men and women. Likewise a woman would receive a higher monthly annuity income from a unisex annuity than she would receive would from a gender-adjusted annuity.

Rates of Return

Annuities are similar to other investment vehicles in that purchasers earn a rate of return on their premium investment. The rate of return on the annuity can be fixed, indexed, variable, or some combination of the three. The risk, regulation and fee structure varies across these different types of annuities.

Table 3. Monthly Income by Gender and Joint/Survivor Option for Fixed Annuity with a $100,000 Premium, 2008

		Unisex	Male	Female
Age 60	Single Life	690	716	666
	Joint and Survivor	645	656	645
Age 65	Single Life	714	801	734
	Joint and Survivor	657	721	707
Age 70	Single Life	869	917	828
	Joint and Survivor	810	811	793

Source: Based on CRS Annuity Calculator. Assumes fixed real (inflation-adjusted) rate of return equal to historical average of 2.8%, and no added adjustments for adverse selection.

A *fixed annuity* pays a fixed monthly payment for the term of the annuity. The amount of the monthly payment is determined at the time the annuity is purchased. The income that any given premium amount will purchase depends mainly on the age of the purchaser (and the age of the purchaser's spouse in the case of a joint and survivor annuity) and prevailing market interest rates for medium-term bonds at the time the annuity is purchased. In 2007, fixed annuities represented 22% of annuity sales.[25]

A *variable annuity* offers annuity purchasers a choice of a wide range of investment options that can vary in value over time. The investment options can include stocks, bonds and money market portfolios. The monthly income provided by a variable annuity will fluctuate according to the investment performance of the funds in which the annuity premium is invested. Income from a variable annuity can decline if the investment underlying the annuity loses value. Some variable annuity policies offer limited protection against declines in value through a guaranteed minimum income. In 2007, the majority of annuity sales (67%) comprised variable annuities.[26]

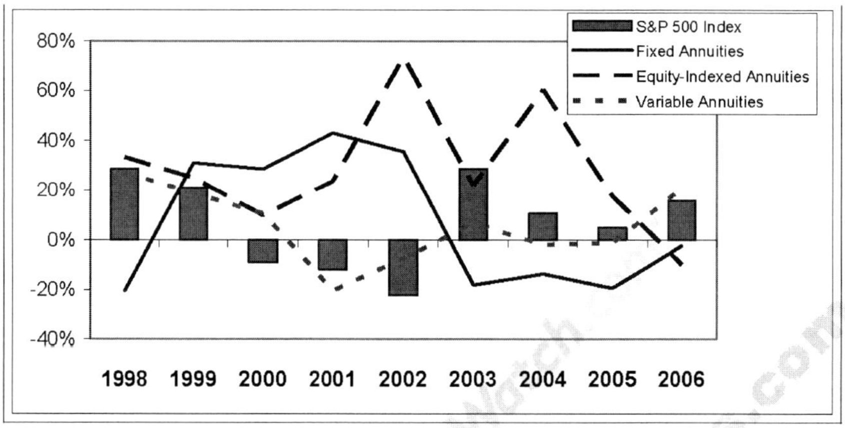

Source: CRS estimates based on data from National Association of Variable Annuity, 2007 Annuity Factbook. Data on growth in equity markets based on annual rate of return of S&P index reported by Ibbotson Associates.

Figure 1. Growth in Annuity Sales Relative to Growth in the S&P 500 Index

An *equity-index* annuity earns a rate of return based on the performance of an equity index fund. Examples of equity indexes used include Dow Jones Industrial Average, Lehman Brothers Aggregate U.S. Index, and Standard and Poor's (S&P) 500 Composite Stock Price Index. If the underlying index declines, the income provided by the annuity will also decline. To reduce this risk, the insurer in some cases may provide a guaranteed minimum payment to protect the consumer against market fluctuations. This minimum, however, costs more to annuity purchasers by reducing their initial annuity income. In 2007, 11% of annuity sales were indexed annuities.[27]

The demand for each type of annuity is influenced by rates of return in equity markets. A strong equity market reduces demand for fixed annuities while a weak stock market increases demand for fixed annuities. During the strong equity market in late 1990s, growth in variable annuities sales exceeded growth in fixed annuity sales. By early 2000, when equity markets were earning negative rates of return, the demand for variable annuities fell. After 2000, growth in variable annuity sales dominated the market. (See **Figure 1**.)

Inflation Protection Options

Inflation-indexed annuities preserve the purchasing power of annuity income by providing a lifetime stream of income that increases with inflation. Treasury Inflation Protected Securities (TIPS) could be used as an investment vehicle by insurers that would like to offer inflation- indexed annuities, but few U.S. insurers offer such annuities. Potential purchasers have proven unwilling to accept a substantially lower initial payment in exchange for protection against inflation. Some insurers offer *graded annuities* that provide annual increases in payments, which are typically capped at 3%, but graded annuities do not fully protect against inflation that exceeds the annual cap.

Tax Treatment of Annuities

The taxation of an annuity differs between the accumulation phase and the payout phase. Deferred annuities receive favorable tax treatment in the accumulation phase. Returns on investment are not taxed in the year they are earned. During the payout phase, taxation of annuity income differs between payments taken as withdrawals and payments taken as a life annuity. In either case, annuity income is taxed at ordinary income tax rates rather than at capital gains tax rates.[28] The taxation of annuity income depends on whether the income is received as

- a single lump sum,
- a series of withdrawals that are not annuitized, or
- a life annuity (either variable or fixed).

When funds are withdrawn as a lump sum, the amount of the distribution that exceeds the amount the annuity owner invested is subject to taxation at the owner's ordinary income tax rate.[29] If money is taken out of the annuity in a series of withdrawals, each withdrawal is considered to consist of investment earnings until all investment gains have been withdrawn.[30] The taxation of annuity income is summarized in **Table 4**.

Taxation of Income from a Fixed Annuity

Each payment from a fixed annuity is treated as consisting partly of the investment gains, which are taxable, and partly as a return of principal, which is not taxable. The proportion of each payment that is excluded from taxable income is determined by dividing the amount that the individual paid into the annuity by the total amount that would be paid out over an average life expectancy, according to life tables published by the Internal Revenue Service. Each payment is multiplied by this ratio to determine the fraction of the annuity payment that is not subject to income taxes. For example, consider an individual who has paid a $100,000 premium for an immediate annuity at age 65. In November 2008, a 65 year-old male would receive monthly income of about $675 for a premium of $100,000. IRS life tables indicate that, on average, the purchaser will receive annuity payments for 20 years.[31] The total expected lifetime income from the annuity therefore would be $162,000.[32] The proportion of each payment that would be excluded from taxable income would be 100,000/162,000, or 61.7%. The other 38.3% percent of each payment would be subject to income taxes.

Taxation of Income from a Variable Annuity

With a variable annuity, income varies with the performance of the underlying investments. The amount of income from a variable annuity that is excluded from taxable income is computed by dividing the premiums paid for the annuity by the number of years that payments are expected to be made to the annuitant. For a life annuity, this would be the annuitant's life expectancy as determined using IRS tables. In the case of a 65 year-old who had paid a premium of $100,000, the amount of each monthly annuity payment that would be excluded from taxable income would be $416.[33]

Table 4. Tax Treatment of Annuities

Type of Account	Individual's Contributions	Investment Returns	Withdrawals
Deferred Annuity	After-tax	Tax-Deferred	Amounts in excess of contributions are taxed as ordinary income
Immediate Annuity	After-tax	Not applicable	Amounts in excess of contributions taxed as ordinary income
Defined Benefit Pension	Varies[a]	Tax-deferred	Amounts not previously included in taxable income taxed as ordinary income

Source: Congressional Research Service.

a. In the private-sector, employee contributions are rarely required. Federal employee pension contributions are made with after-tax income. Tax treatment of pension contribution by state and local employees varies by locality.

Tax Exclusion for Long-Term Care Insurance

An exception to the taxation of annuity income was included in the Pension Protection Act of 2006 (P.L. 109-280). Beginning in 2010, withdrawals from annuity contracts that are used to pay for qualified long-term care insurance premiums are not subject to income tax. However, the investment in the annuity contract is reduced by the amount of the long-term care insurance premiums. This means that a larger percentage of the future income received from the annuity will represent investment gains and will be subject to income taxes.

Consumer Protections and the Regulatory Environment

Consumer protections are intended to ensure that information used to sell an annuity is truthful, and that individuals who purchase an annuity fully understand the future consequences with respect to retirement income. The key challenge in the development and enforcement of consumer protections is that some annuity products are regulated exclusively at the state level while others are also regulated by federal agencies. Because state governments have primary jurisdiction over regulation of fixed annuities, there is wide variation in regulation across states. Further, while variable annuities are regulated by the federal Securities and Exchange Commission (SEC), equity-index annuities, which are designed to track the performance of a common stock index, such as the S&P 500 or the Russell 2000, are regulated primarily by the states.

State Regulation of Annuities

Like other insurance products, most annuities are regulated by the states. State laws govern the organization and licensing of insurance companies and their agents and state insurance departments oversee insurance company operations. These state laws and regulations also govern marketing and sales practices as well as insurer requirements.

To help guide states in their oversight efforts, the National Association of Insurance Commissioners (NAIC) has developed language for "model laws and regulations" to provide guidelines for legislators to modify and adopt in their respective states. The NAIC Model Act has not been uniformly adopted across states, thus leaving potential gaps in consumer protections. As of February 2008, 17 states have not adopted the NAIC model regulations on suitability.[34] The NAIC Model Suitability language requires insurance companies to give objective financial information to potential purchasers, and it requires agents to use a standardized form to determine whether an annuity would be suitable for the potential purchaser. Some state laws ban the use of professional designations or titles – such as Senior Financial Advisor – that might mislead senior consumers into thinking the advisor has special financial expertise related to the needs of older consumers.

A similar problem exists with respect to disclosure requirements in annuity contracts. The NAIC Annuity Disclosure Model Regulation requires certain information to be disclosed, including information about premiums and how they are charged, a summary of the options and restrictions for accessing money, and an outline of fees. According to the NAIC, 35 states have adopted the NAIC disclosure regulation.

The states also play a role in protecting annuity owners against the insolvency of annuity insurers. To do this, each state has a state guaranty association to provide a financial safety net for each line of insurance and to ensure that coverage continues if an insurer becomes insolvent. State laws require insurers to become members of the guaranty associations in every state in which they are licensed to do business. The actual coverage for annuity contracts varies from state to state, but cash values and annuity benefits are usually protected up to at least $100,000. However, coverage is not provided for variable annuity contracts. Variable annuity contracts are held in separate accounts by insurers and they are protected from the general creditors of the insurance company in the event of insolvency. Although the Securities Investor Protection Corporation (SIPC) protects against fraud in variable annuity sales, it does not provide any relief to investors whose variable annuities decline due to falling prices in equity markets.

Federal Regulation of Annuities

Because the assets underlying variable annuities are invested in equities, they are also regulated by the federal government through the Securities and Exchange Commission (SEC). Equity-index annuities, which are based on market indexes, are now regulated by the SEC (see discussion below). Federal securities laws require certain disclosure documents, including a prospectus, to be given to investors. Certain disclosure documents must also be filed with the SEC. In addition, written marketing materials, such as advertisements, are subject to federal regulation.

Federal law prohibits agents who sell variable annuities from making untrue statements of material fact or failing to state a material fact that is necessary to prevent the statement from being misleading.[35] Annuity agents also have a fiduciary duty to provide full and fair disclosure of all material facts to their clients and their prospective clients, including all statements in advertising materials. Up until 2009, equity-index annuities were regulated by the states, rather then the SEC. To address this inconsistency in regulation between variable and equity-index annuities, the Securities and Exchange Commission has finalized regulations on January 16, 2009, that would extend federal securities laws with respect to full and fair disclosure and sales practice protections to certain equity-index annuities.[36]

Why Is Demand for Individual Annuities So Low?

Despite some of the potential advantages of individual life annuities, immediate annuities remain a small part of retirement assets held in the U.S. Of those who purchased immediate annuities in 2003, the median age of purchase was 70.[37] The Internal Revenue Code requires owners of individual retirement accounts to begin taking withdrawals from their accounts and including the withdrawals in their taxable income no later than April of the year in which they reach age 70½. Some owners of IRAs use immediate annuities to meet the requirement to take these "required minimum distributions" from their retirement accounts. Without this requirement, demand for annuities might even be lower.

There are several reasons why the demand for annuities is low despite the aging of the population. Some potential purchasers may already feel they have a sufficient amount of annuitized income from Social Security, and about a third of people 65 and older also have annuity income from defined benefit pensions. Another reason may be the amount and non- transparency of fees and expenses charged by insurance companies. Further, annuity contracts are not easily canceled, and many individuals fear that after purchasing an annuity they may later need a large sum of money to pay for unexpected expenses, such as long-term care or health expenses. Even among people who understand that it is important to insure against longevity risk, some fear that they will die before reaching their normal life expectancy, and will end up "losing the bet" with the insurance company that sold the annuity. Finally, recent adverse publicity about deceptive sales practices in the annuity market has added to concerns among potential buyers of immediate annuities.

Complexity and Lack of Transparency in Annuity Expenses

Annuity providers impose a number of fees and expenses that are complex and are not transparent to the annuity purchaser. Even a rather "simple" prospectus identifying the various fees can be more than 50 pages long.[38]

Fees and expenses fall into three main categories: surrender charges, investment fees, and insurance charges. Fees and expenses vary depending on the type of annuity (fixed or variable). Both fixed and variable annuities have surrender charges, which are fees for cancelling the contract before a specified number of years have passed. A typical surrender charge starts at 7% of the premium in the first year of the contract and declines by 1% a year until it reaches zero. However, a few companies have surrender charges of up to 15% to 25% of the annuity premium.[39]

Variable annuities have two additional fees associated with managing assets. These are investment management fees and insurance charges. Investment management fees cover the cost of managing the different funds across investment accounts. Investment fees vary depending on the type of investment portfolio chosen. Insurance charges include administration, sales commissions, and mortality and expense charges. Mortality and expense charges average 1.15% of the average value of investment and cover three components of the insurance guarantee:

- Mortality premium or guarantee of income over one's lifetime;
- Death benefit to protect beneficiaries (also called survivor benefit); and,
- The cost of the minimum income guarantee.

These fees vary by product design. Typically, a fixed annuity with a joint and survivor option is subject to all three components. However, a variable annuity without a joint and survivor option and no minimum guarantee would only be subject to the mortality premium.

It is difficult for consumers to identify and understand each fee charged for an annuity. Each insurer has a different format for disclosing information. The insurance industry has recognized this problem and has begun to standardize fee disclosure. A group of insurance organizations is working to develop a simple, standardized disclosure document that presents information about fees in a consumer-friendly manner.[40]

Another factor affecting the cost of annuities is that people who buy annuities tend to be those who expect to live longer than average. A person who chooses to purchase an annuity may have information about his or her health, habits, or family history that the insurance company does not have regarding their risk of living longer than average. This phenomenon, called "adverse selection," leads to higher annuity premiums than insurers would otherwise have to charge if longevity risk were spread over the entire population. Estimates of the cost of adverse selection vary. Some studies have found that adverse selection reduces income to annuity purchasers by 4 cents to 10 cents per dollar of premiums paid.[41] A more recent study defined "potential annuitants" more narrowly to only include those with sufficient wealth to purchase an annuity. When re-defined in this manner, potential annuitants tend to live considerably longer than average and thus would receive a better deal from an annuity than the average person. According to this analysis, the impact of adverse selection on annuity prices is only about half as great as previously estimated, or about 2 cents to 5 cents per premium dollar.[42] If participation in individual annuities were broader, the effect of adverse selection would be reduced and annuitants' income would be higher.

Lack of Flexibility in Dealing with Unexpected Expenses

Once an individual purchases an immediate annuity, the decision is not easily reversible. Most states require a 10-day look back period during which a buyer can change his or her mind, but after this, canceling an annuity contract will result in substantial surrender charges. Part of the lack of flexibility in annuity contracts was recently addressed in the Pension Protection Act of 2006, which allows funds used to purchase an annuity to be withdrawn tax-free to buy long-term care insurance. It is important to note that long-term care insurance must be purchased well in advance of actually needing long-term care services. Annuity owners would have to make the decision to purchase long-term care insurance in the early years of the payout phase.

Dying Before Getting Full Value. Annuity buyers pay for the insurance component of the annuity, which guarantees a monthly income no matter how long the annuitant lives. Some people are reluctant to purchase an annuity out of fear that they will die before they get back the premiums that they paid into it. Joint and survivor annuities and term-certain annuities can assure that annuity payments will continue even if the purchaser dies earlier than he or she expected, but these options reduce the monthly payments that the annuitant receives while he or she is living.

Adverse Publicity and Lack of Knowledge About Annuities. Another factor affecting current demand for annuities may be adverse publicity surrounding false advertising and deceptive sales practices employed by insurance agents selling equity-index annuities. These practices may have led some consumers to avoid all annuity products. Equity-index annuities, however, currently account for only 11% of annuity sales. Further, recent proposals by the SEC to strengthen regulations for sales of equity-index annuities may help to alleviate consumers' concerns in the future.

RETIREMENT ACCOUNT WITHDRAWAL STRATEGIES

Although annuities offer protection from longevity risk and investment risk, relatively few people use their retirement savings to purchase an annuity. Most people choose instead to take periodic withdrawals from their retirement accounts. Individuals who purchase life annuities transfer the responsibility for managing assets and the risk of outliving their assets to an insurance company. In contrast, retirees who "self-annuitize" take on the responsibility of managing their investments and also the risk of living longer than average. Annuity purchasers, however, give up control over the assets that they use to purchase their annuities, while those who take periodic withdrawals have the money in their retirement accounts available to meet large, unexpected expenses that may arise during retirement.

For those who choose to take periodic withdrawals, there are two basic approaches to taking money out of their retirement accounts. The first approach attempts to "smooth" consumption over the period of retirement through equal (inflation-adjusted) withdrawals each year. This method provides a steady income from year to year, but as the examples presented in this report will illustrate, it can be difficult to choose a rate of withdrawal that can be sustained in the face of uncertain life expectancy and variable rates of return on investment. Another strategy for drawing down retirement assets is to take withdrawals that are based on the individual's remaining life expectancy in the year that each withdrawal is taken. This method of withdrawing money from a retirement account is prescribed by law for the *required minimum distributions* that all owners of traditional IRAs and retired owners of 401(k) accounts must begin taking after they reach age $70^1/2$.[43] Under this approach, it is unlikely that the individual will exhaust his or her savings, but withdrawals can vary substantially from year to year. This can make planning and budgeting difficult.

An individual who chooses to take periodic withdrawals might want to have some idea how likely his or her chosen strategy is to succeed. The first step in such an assessment is to define success. Financial planners often advise clients that they should adopt a method of withdrawing retirement funds that will result in a high probability that their savings will last 30 to 40 years. Assuming that 40 years is a reasonable upper bound for the number of years that a retirement account might need to last, the next task for the retiree is to determine the minimum probability of success that he or she is willing to accept. There is no fixed standard for the minimum probability of success that a retiree should be willing to accept for the annual rate of withdrawal that he or she chooses. For purposes of illustration, we have highlighted in the tables that follow the combinations of initial withdrawal rates and investment allocations that resulted in an account balance lasting for a given number of years (or to a given age) in 95.0% or more of our simulations.

How Long Will a Retirement Account Last with Fixed Annual Withdrawals?

One way to evaluate the likely success of a withdrawal strategy is to determine the probability that the retiree's assets will last for at least a specific number of years, assuming that rates of return on investment will vary from year to year. To estimate this probability, CRS developed a model that estimates how long a sum of money will last, assuming a particular initial rate of withdrawal and the probable distribution of annual rates of return on investment. The model estimates the annual rate of return on investment through a Monte Carlo simulation process in which the rate of return in each year is based on the distribution of annual total returns on stocks and bonds over the 82 years from 1926 through 2007.[44] (See **Appendix A** for a description of Monte Carlo simulation processes.)

It is important to note that an annual rate of withdrawal that minimizes the risk of exhausting a retirement account – whether by delaying the initial withdrawal or by taking "small" annual withdrawals – will increase the likelihood that the account will have substantial assets remaining at the time of the owner's death. Delaying the initial withdrawal and taking relatively small withdrawals both help to preserve assets in the event that the individual outlives his or her normal life expectancy or experiences below-average rates of investment return. However, for the individual who lives to his or her normal life expectancy and experiences average rates of return on investment, the end result of successfully reducing the risk of exhausting his or her account may be a substantial unexpended account balance at the time of death.

Initial Rate of Withdrawal

CRS estimated the probability that assets would last for five periods of time ranging from 20 years to 40 years at five initial withdrawal rates ranging from 4.0% to 6.0% of the value of the account when the first withdrawal is taken. We chose this range of withdrawal rates because "a large body of research on 'safe' withdrawal rates for individuals has determined that a real withdrawal rate in the neighborhood of 4 percent of the initial retirement portfolio has a 'low' chance of running out of money,"[45] and because recent research has demonstrated that initial rates of withdrawal equal to 7.0% or more are very likely to exhaust the assets too rapidly.[46] In the estimates presented in the following tables, the withdrawal rate is stated as the percentage of the *initial* withdrawal from the account. Subsequent withdrawals are equal to the first withdrawal in constant (inflation-adjusted) dollars, but they may represent a different percentage of the remaining account balance.[47]

Investment Portfolio

Many financial advisors recommend that retirees should keep 50% or more of their retirement savings invested in a diversified portfolio of stocks because stocks have historically achieved a higher long-run average rate of return than bonds. The higher long-run average rate of return on common stocks compared to bonds acts as a form of longevity insurance for the retiree. Generally, advisors recommend that the remainder of assets should be invested in bonds and money market securities that are less susceptible than stocks to large capital losses.

In our analysis, we simulated withdrawals from two portfolios. In one set of simulations, retirees allocated 65% of assets to the ***Standard & Poor's 500*** index of stocks and invested the remainder in AAA-rated corporate bonds. In the second set of simulations, retirees allocated 35% of assets to the *Standard & Poor 's 500* index of stocks and invested the remainder in AAA-rated corporate bonds. In all of the simulations, withdrawals were taken at the beginning of each year. Accounts were re-balanced annually so that the portfolio would start each year at the chosen allocation between stocks and bonds. The model also took into account the correlation between annual returns on stocks and bonds.[48] The effects of account fees and income taxes were ignored for purposes of this analysis.[49]

Probability of Assets Lasting for at Least a Specific Number of Years

The data presented in **Table 5** illustrate the likelihood that savings will last for at least a given number of years under several initial rates of withdrawal and under the two investment portfolios described above. Panel 1 of **Table 5** shows the probability that a retirement account will last for at least a given number of years, assuming that 65% of the assets in the account are invested in stocks represented by the *Standard & Poor's 500* index and 35% of the assets are invested in AAA-rated corporate bonds. Panel 2 of **Table 5** shows the probability that savings will last for at least a given length of time, assuming that 35% of the assets are invested in stocks and 65% of the assets are invested in bonds.[50]

Portfolio of 65% Stocks and 35% Bonds

The results presented in **Table 5** indicate that at an initial withdrawal rate of 4.0%, there is a 98.5% probability that an account invested in this portfolio will last for at least 20 years. The longer the period of time over which withdrawals are taken, the lower the likelihood that a given rate of withdrawal will continue to be successful. At a 4.0% initial rate of withdrawal, there is a 92.5% chance that the account will last for 30 years or more, and an 86.8% chance that it will last for at least 40 years.

Table 5. Estimated Probability a Retirement Account Will Last for at Least a Specific Number of Years

Probability that Money Will Last:	**Initial Annual Withdrawal from Retirement Account**				
	4.0%	**4.5%**	**5.0%**	**5.5%**	**6.0%**
Panel 1: Investment Portfolio = 65% Stocks, 35% Bonds					
20 years or more	*98.5*	*96.9*	94.1	89.8	84.2
25 years or more	*95.7*	92.3	87.0	80.7	72.3
30 years or more	92.5	87.2	80.5	72.6	63.3
35 years or more	89.6	82.7	75.3	66.4	56.3
40 years or more	86.8	78.3	71.0	61.7	51.4
Panel 2: Investment Portfolio = 35% Stocks, 65% Bonds Probability that money will last:					
20 years or more	*99.7*	*98.9*	*96.4*	92.2	84.8
25 years or more	97.7	94.5	87.8	78.3	65.2
30 years or more	94.0	87.3	77.0	64.1	49.5
35 years or more	89.4	79.7	66.9	53.2	38.8
40 years or more	84.3	73.2	58.9	45.6	31.1

Source: Congressional Research Service.

Notes: Probabilities >= 95.0% are in italics.

For any given number of years, the likelihood of an account lasting for at least that length of time is lower for higher initial rates of withdrawal. While there is a 98.5% chance that an account will last for at least 20 years at a 4.0% initial rate of withdrawal, this probability drops to 94.1% for a 5.0% initial rate of withdrawal and to 84.2% for a 6.0% initial rate of withdrawal.

Portfolio of 35% Stocks and 65% Bonds

Panel 2 of **Table 5** shows the probability that a retirement account in which 35% of assets are invested in stocks and 65% of assets are invested in bonds would last for at least 20, 30, or 40 years. The results of the simulations indicate that for periods of time of 20 years or more, the likelihood of exhausting a retirement account is higher for an account with a 65% allocation to bonds compared to an account with a 65% allocation to stocks.

The likelihood that an account would last for at least 20 years is slightly higher for an account with a 65% allocation to bonds compared to an account with a 65% allocation to stocks. This result occurs because a portfolio that is more heavily invested in stocks has a greater chance than a portfolio mainly invested in bonds of experiencing a large capital loss. If this happens in the early years of retirement, the account may be depleted rapidly. Over longer periods of time, however, the probability of running out of money is substantially higher with a portfolio in which 65% of assets are invested in bonds compared to a portfolio in which 65% of assets are invested in stocks because of the lower expected average annual rate of return on bonds.

Estimates Incorporating Life Expectancy

The estimates presented in **Table 5** illustrate the probability that a retirement account will last for at least a given number of years, assuming a particular initial rate of withdrawal, a specific allocation of investments between stocks and bonds, and the estimated annual rates of return on investment. These results are likely to underestimate the likelihood that a particular strategy will succeed because they do not account for individual mortality. Because not all account owners will live until the end of a fixed interval of time, the probability of an account having money in it at the *earlier* of either the account owner's death or the end of the interval is greater than the probability of the account having money in it at the end of the interval. To ignore the possibility of the account owner dying in any year will result in underestimating the probability that a particular rate of withdrawal will sustain the account throughout the owner's lifetime. As other researchers have noted, the relevant consideration in planning retirement withdrawals is "the probability of running out of money in the retirement life span, whether that span is shorter or longer than a predetermined number of years."[51]

Estimates of the likelihood that a retirement account will last for a particular number of years should include the probability that the account owner will survive for that number of years. This can be done by including in the model of retirement withdrawals the probability of the individual surviving from one year to the next. To incorporate the effect of mortality on the probability that a retiree will exhaust his or her retirement account before the earlier of either the retiree's death or the attainment of a particular age, CRS added two variables to its model. One variable accounts for the individual's age at retirement and in each succeeding year, and the other makes each annual withdrawal conditional on the individual having survived from one year to the next.[52] The probability of survival from year to year was based on male and female life expectancies taken from cohort life tables.[53] An individual's withdrawal strategy was considered to have been successful if there was a 95.0% or higher probability that he or she had a positive account balance in the year of death or, if still living, at the ages of 80, 85, 90, 95, and 100.

Table 6, Table 7, and **Table 8** show the estimated probabilities that the retirement accounts of men and women who retire at ages 60, 65, or 70 will last until the ages of 80, 85, 90, 95, and 100, taking into account the probability of the individual dying in each year.[54] The initial withdrawal rates range from 4.0% to 6.0% and subsequent withdrawals are assumed to be equal in real value (i.e., adjusted for inflation) to the initial withdrawal.[55] The tables show the estimated probabilities of success for two portfolios. In one portfolio, 65% of assets are invested in stocks and 35% in bonds, and in the other portfolio, 65% of assets are invested in bonds and 35% in stocks.

The data presented in **Table 6** show the estimated probabilities of a retirement account lasting until ages 80, 85, 90, 95, and 100 for men and women retiring at age 60. **Table 5** showed that at a 4.0% initial rate of withdrawal from an account invested 65% in stocks and 35% in bonds, there is a 98.5% chance that a retirement account will last for at least 20 years. The results presented in **Table 6** show that under the same set of assumptions, but incorporating the effects of mortality, a man retiring at 60 has a 99.1% chance that his retirement account will last until at least age 80, while for a woman retiring at age 60 there is a 98.9% chance that her account will last until at least age 80. In this case, the probabilities are almost equally high in both **Table 5** and **Table 6**, and there is little difference in the probabilities of success between and women. Both of these results change for the probability of success at later ages.

Table 5 showed that at a 4.0% withdrawal rate, the probability of a retirement account lasting for at least 30 years was 92.5%. The data in **Table 6** show that once the effects of mortality are taken into consideration, there is a 97.3% chance that a man who retires at 60 and takes an initial withdrawal of 4.0%, will still have some money in the account at age 90, while a woman retiring at age 60 and taking an initial withdrawal of 4.0% has a 96.1% chance of still having money in her account on her 90th birthday. The probability that a woman will still have money in her account at any given age is lower than the probability for a man because a woman has a higher probability of having survived to that age. (See **Appendix B**.)

In simulations representing retirement at age 60, a withdrawal rate of 4.0% was successful in 95.0% or more of simulations for both men and women under both investment portfolios at all ages up to 100. (See **Table 6**.) A withdrawal rate of 6.0% failed to achieve a 95.0% success rate for either men or women under either investment portfolio even just to age 80. For both men and women retiring at age 60, a withdrawal rate of 5.0% or higher carries a high risk that their retirement accounts will be exhausted before they have attained their normal life expectancies.

Table 7 and **Table 8** show that, compared to retiring at age 60, delaying retirement until 65 or 70 can substantially increase the likelihood that an individual will not exhaust his or her retirement account before he or she dies. In simulations representing retirement at age 65, withdrawal rates of 4.0% and 4.5% were successful in 95.0% or more of simulations for both men and women under both investment portfolios at all ages up to 100. (See **Table 7**.) A withdrawal rate of 6.0% achieved a 95.0% success rate under either investment portfolio for both men and women only up to age 80. For men who retire at age 65, a withdrawal rate of 5.5% or higher carries a substantial risk that their retirement accounts will be exhausted if they live to age 90 or older. For women who retire at age 65, a withdrawal rate of 5.0% or higher carries a substantial risk that their retirement accounts will be exhausted if they live to age 90 or older.

In simulations representing retirement at age 70, withdrawal rates of 4.0%, 4.5%, and 5.0% were successful in 95.0% or more of simulations for both men and women under both investment portfolios at all ages up to 100. (See **Table 8.**) A withdrawal rate of 5.5% was successful up to age 100 in 94.7% or more of cases for men under either investment portfolio, but succeeded in 95.0% or more of cases only to age 90 for women. For men who retire at age 70, a withdrawal rate of 6.0% or higher carries a substantial risk that their retirement accounts will be exhausted if they live to age 95 or older. For women who retire at age 70, a withdrawal rate of 5.5% or higher carries a substantial risk that their retirement accounts will be exhausted if they live to age 95 or older.

Table 6. Probability of Retirement Account Lasting to at Least a Given Age, Including Mortality Risk, Retirement at Age 60

Probability that Money Will Last at Least Until:	**Initial Annual Withdrawal from Retirement Account**				
	4.0%	**4.5%**	**5.0%**	**5.5%**	**6.0%**
Panel 1: Male Retiring at Age 60, Portfolio = 65% Stocks, 35% Bonds					
Age 80	*99.1*	*98.1*	*96.4*	93.5	89.8
Age 85	*98.1*	*96.3*	93.2	89.6	84.8
Age 90	*97.3*	*95.0*	91.4	87.3	82.6
Age 95	*97.0*	94.4	90.6	86.4	81.9
Age 100	*96.9*	94.3	90.5	86.3	81.7
Panel 2: Male Retiring at Age 60, Portfolio = 35% Stocks, 65% Bonds					
Age 80	*99.8*	*99.4*	*98.1*	95.1	90.8
Age 85	*99.1*	*97.6*	94.1	89.1	82.5
Age 90	*98.1*	*95.8*	91.4	85.6	78.6
Age 95	*97.7*	*95.0*	90.4	84.3	77.1
Age 100	*97.5*	94.8	90.1	84.1	76.9
Panel 3: Female Retiring at Age 60, Portfolio = 65% Stocks, 35% Bonds					
Age 80	*98.9*	*97.8*	*95.5*	92.7	88.3
Age 85	*97.5*	*95.6*	91.6	87.0	81.7
Age 90	*96.1*	93.6	89.0	83.7	78.3
Age 95	*95.5*	92.8	87.7	82.5	77.0
Age 100	*95.3*	92.6	87.4	82.2	76.6
Panel 4: Female Retiring at Age 60, Portfolio = 35% Stocks, 65% Bonds					
Age 80	*99.7*	*99.2*	*97.5*	94.4	88.6
Age 85	*98.4*	*96.7*	92.8	86.9	77.7
Age 90	*96.9*	94.3	88.2	81.2	71.7
Age 95	*96.1*	92.8	86.1	78.9	69.4
Age 100	*95.7*	92.3	85.4	78.4	69.0

Source: Congressional Research Service.

Notes: Probabilities >= 95.0% are in italics.

Table 7. Probability of Retirement Account Lasting to at Least a Given Age, Including Mortality Risk, Retirement at Age 65

Probability that Money Will Last at Least Until:	**Initial Annual Withdrawal from Retirement Account**				
	4.0%	**4.5%**	**5.0%**	**5.5%**	**6.0%**
Panel 1: Male Retiring at Age 65, Portfolio = 65% Stocks, 35% Bonds					
Age 80	*99.9*	*99.7*	*99.3*	*98.6*	*96.9*
Age 85	*99.3*	*98.4*	*97.3*	*95.1*	91.9
Age 90	*98.7*	*97.0*	*95.5*	92.6	88.5
Age 95	*98.3*	*96.4*	94.8	91.6	87.3
Age 100	*98.1*	*96.2*	94.6	91.4	87.1
Panel 2: Male Retiring at Age 65, Portfolio = 35% Stocks, 65% Bonds					
Age 80	*>99.9*	*>99.9*	*>99.9*	*99.6*	*98.7*
Age 85	*99.8*	*99.5*	*98.5*	*96.6*	92.5
Age 90	*99.3*	*98.2*	*96.2*	92.8	87.3
Age 95	*98.9*	*97.4*	*95.0*	91.3	85.5
Age 100	*98.7*	*97.1*	94.6	90.9	85.1
Panel 3: Female Retiring at Age 65, Portfolio = 65% Stocks, 35% Bonds					
Age 80	*99.9*	*99.7*	*99.1*	*98.2*	*97.0*
Age 85	*99.0*	*98.1*	*96.3*	93.8	90.9
Age 90	*97.8*	*96.3*	93.5	89.7	86.0
Age 95	*97.1*	*95.5*	92.2	87.8	83.9
Age 100	*96.9*	*95.1*	91.8	87.4	83.4
Panel 4: Female Retiring at Age 65, Portfolio = 35% Stocks, 65% Bonds					
Age 80	*>99.9*	*>99.9*	*99.9*	*99.5*	*98.3*
Age 85	*99.9*	*99.2*	*98.1*	*95.5*	90.9
Age 90	*99.1*	*97.3*	94.3	90.1	82.9
Age 95	*98.3*	*95.7*	92.1	87.3	79.6
Age 100	*98.0*	*95.2*	91.2	86.4	78.8

Source: Congressional Research Service.

Notes: Probabilities >= 95.0% are in italics.

Estimates of Variable Annual Withdrawals

The estimates shown in **Table 5, Table 6, Table 7,** and **Table 8** are based on simulations of a withdrawal strategy that produces annual income of a constant real (inflation-adjusted) amount. The individual takes an initial annual withdrawal equal to a particular percentage of the account balance, and all subsequent withdrawals are equal to the real value of the initial withdrawal. In this respect, the withdrawal strategy mimics an inflation-indexed annuity by providing a steady annual income.[56] However, an individual who self-annuitizes must, in effect, insure against his or her own longevity by holding substantial "reserves" in the account to protect against the possibility of outliving his or her savings. Because insurers diversify the risk of longevity over all annuity purchasers, they are able to pay a higher annual income than an individual who selfannuitizes could safely withdraw from his or her account. Taking withdrawals from a retirement account that are equal to the amount that would be paid by an annuity purchased from an insurance company exposes the retiree to the risk of outliving his assets.[57]

Table 8. Probability of Retirement Account Lasting to at Least a Given Age, Including Mortality Risk, Retirement at Age 70

Probability that Money Will Last at Least Until:	Initial Annual Withdrawal from Retirement Account				
	4.0%	**4.5%**	**5.0%**	**5.5%**	**6.0%**
Panel 1: Male Retiring at Age 70, Portfolio = 65% Stocks, 35% Bonds					
Age 80	*>99.9*	*>99.9*	*>99.9*	*99.9*	*99.9*
Age 85	*>99.9*	*99.8*	*99.4*	*98.5*	*97.9*
Age 90	*99.7*	*99.0*	*98.1*	*96.2*	94.5
Age 95	*99.4*	*98.4*	*97.4*	*95.0*	92.9
Age 100	*99.3*	*98.1*	*97.1*	94.7	92.6
Panel 2: Male Retiring at Age 70, Portfolio = 35% Stocks, 65% Bonds					
Age 80	*>99.9*	*>99.9*	*>99.9*	*>99.9*	*>99.9*
Age 85	*>99.9*	*>99.9*	*99.9*	*99.6*	*99.0*
Age 90	*99.9*	*99.7*	*98.9*	*97.6*	*95.2*
Age 95	*99.6*	*99.1*	*97.7*	*95.6*	92.4
Age 100	*99.5*	*98.8*	*97.2*	*95.1*	91.7
Panel 3: Female Retiring at Age 70, Portfolio = 65% Stocks, 35% Bonds					
Age 80	*>99.9*	*>99.9*	*>99.9*	*>99.9*	*99.9*
Age 85	*99.9*	*99.7*	*99.4*	*98.6*	*97.7*
Age 90	*99.5*	*98.6*	*97.4*	*95.2*	93.1
Age 95	*98.8*	*97.6*	*95.9*	93.3	90.6
Age 100	*98.5*	*97.2*	*95.3*	92.6	89.9
Panel 4: Female Retiring at Age 70, Portfolio = 35% Stocks, 65% Bonds					
Age 80	*>99.9*	*>99.9*	*>99.9*	*>99.9*	*>99.9*
Age 85	*>99.9*	*99.9*	*99.9*	*99.6*	*99.0*
Age 90	*99.9*	*99.4*	*98.5*	*96.5*	93.2
Age 95	*99.4*	*98.4*	*96.6*	93.4	88.7
Age 100	*99.1*	*97.9*	*95.7*	92.3	87.6

Source: Congressional Research Service.

Notes: Probabilities >= 95.0% are in italics.

If a retiree is willing to allow the amount withdrawn from the account to vary from year to year based on investment returns and remaining life expectancy, he or she can reduce the likelihood of fully depleting the account before dying. The trade-off for reducing this risk is that the individual's annual income will be less predictable. This can make planning and budgeting more difficult. One such strategy bases each annual withdrawal on the current account balance and the individual's remaining life expectancy.[58] This withdrawal rule is mandated under the Internal Revenue Code for owners of traditional IRAs and retired owners of 401(k) plans after they attain age 70½ "to ensure that retirees consume their tax-qualified retirement pension accounts instead of leaving them as bequests for their heirs."[59]

Table 9, **Table 10**, and **Table 11** show how annual withdrawals that are based on the individual's remaining life expectancy in the year that the withdrawal is taken can vary over the course of the person's retirement. **Table 9** illustrates the variability of withdrawals for a man and a woman each of whom retires at age 60 with an account balance of $100,000. **Table 10** and **Table 11** show withdrawals for men and women who retire at ages 65 and 70, respectively, also with initial account balances of $100,000.[60] In 2004, a 60 year-old man had a remaining life expectancy of 20.8 years and a woman had a remaining life expectancy of 24.0 years.[61] Under the $1/E(t)$ withdrawal rule, the 60 year-old man would withdraw 1/20.8 (4.8%) of his account balance and the 60 year-old woman would withdraw 1/24.0 (4.2%) of her account. One year later, the 61 year- old man would have a remaining life expectancy of 20.0 years and would withdraw 1/20.0 (5.0%) of his account balance. The 61 year-old woman would have a remaining life expectancy of 23.2 years and would withdraw 1/23.2 (4.3%) of her account balance. As the retiree ages, his or her remaining life expectancy falls, and the percentage of the account that he or she withdraws rises. At age 75, for example, a man has a remaining life expectancy of 10.7 years and so he would withdraw 1/10.7 (9.3%) of his remaining account balance. A 75 year-old woman has a remaining life expectancy of 12.8 years and would withdraw 1/12.8 (7.8%) of her remaining account balance.

Under this method, annual withdrawals are a continually rising fraction of the remaining account balance, but the real dollar of value of the withdrawals may rise or fall from year to year, depending on the investment performance of the retirement account. In a "worst-case scenario" the aging retiree's withdrawals would be a rising fraction of a shrinking account balance. Although the retiree would not fully deplete the account—because the withdrawal is never equal to 100% of the remaining account balance—if the account shrinks in value due to a decline in asset values, the withdrawals could grow smaller from year to year.[62]

Withdrawals based on remaining life expectancy will vary in size (measured here in constant dollars) from year to year. For example, the top panel of **Table 9** shows the range of withdrawals taken between the ages of 60 and 100 by a man who retires at age 60 with an account balance of $100,000. Across 10,000 simulations, the typical male retiree could expect his annual withdrawals to range from $4,465 to $9,160 with an average withdrawal of $6,394. In 5% of the simulations, however, the *smallest* annual withdrawal was $1,409 or less, and in 5% of the simulations, the *largest* withdrawal was $22,803 or more. A woman with the same portfolio retiring at age 60 could expect her annual withdrawals to range from $3,940 to $9,729 with an average withdrawal of $6,342. (See Panel 3 of **Table 9**. In 5% of the simulations, the smallest annual withdrawal was $1,530 or less, and in 5% of the simulations, the largest withdrawal was $25,968 or more.

Table 9. Variable Annual Withdrawals Based on Life Expectancy, Retirement at Age 60 (account balance at age 60 = $100,000)

	Annual Withdrawal Based on Remaining Life Expectancy		
	5th Percentile	**Median**	**95th Percentile**
Panel 1: Male Retiring at Age 60, Portfolio = 65% Stocks, 35% Bonds			
Smallest withdrawal	1,409	**4,465**	4,818
Mean withdrawal	3,857	**6,394**	12,781
Largest withdrawal	4,818	**9,160**	22,803
Panel 2: Male Retiring at Age 60, Portfolio = 35% Stocks, 65% Bonds			
Smallest withdrawal	1,100	**4,491**	4,818
Mean withdrawal	3,978	**5,734**	8,845
Largest withdrawal	4,818	**7,370**	13,184
Panel 3: Female Retiring at Age 60, Portfolio = 65% Stocks, 35% Bonds			
Smallest withdrawal	1,530	**3,940**	4,168
Mean withdrawal	3,589	**6,342**	13,638
Largest withdrawal	4,378	**9,729**	25,968
Panel 4: Female Retiring at Age 60, Portfolio = 35% Stocks, 65% Bonds			
Smallest withdrawal	1,349	**3,985**	4,168
Mean withdrawal	3,729	**5,516**	9,061
Largest withdrawal	4,311	**7,465**	14,460

Source: Congressional Research Service.

Panels 2 and 4 of **Table 9** show that when the simulations were based on a portfolio in which 65% of assets were invested in bonds and 35% invested in stocks, the average withdrawal was smaller than in the case of the more stock-heavy portfolio. The typical male retiring at 60 with a $100,000 portfolio invested 65% in bonds and 35% in stocks could expect his annual withdrawals to range from $4,491 to $7,370 with an average withdrawal of $5,734. (Again, all amounts are in constant dollars.) In 5% of all the simulations, however, the smallest annual withdrawal was $1,100 or less, and in 5% of the simulations, the largest withdrawal was $13,184 or more. A woman with the same portfolio who retires at age 60 could expect her annual withdrawals to range from $3,985 to $7,465, with an average withdrawal of $5,516. (See Panel 4 of **Table 9**.) In 5% of all the simulations, the smallest annual withdrawal was $1,349 or less, and in 5% of the simulations, the largest withdrawal was $14,460 or more.

Table 10. Variable Annual Withdrawals Based on Life Expectancy, Retirement at Age 65 (account balance at age 65 = $100,000)

	Annual Withdrawal Based on Remaining Life Expectancy		
	5th Percentile	**Median**	**95th Percentile**
Panel 1: Male Retiring at Age 65, Portfolio = 65% Stocks, 35% Bonds			
Smallest withdrawal	1,460	**5,284**	5,851
Mean withdrawal	4,331	**6,861**	12,146
Largest withdrawal	5,851	**9,103**	19,513
Panel 2: Male Retiring at Age 65, Portfolio = 35% Stocks, 65% Bonds			
Smallest withdrawal	1,146	**5,210**	5,851
Mean withdrawal	4,442	**6,270**	9,025
Largest withdrawal	5,851	**7,689**	12,572
Panel 3: Female retiring at Age 65, portfolio = 65% Stocks, 35% Bonds			
Smallest withdrawal	1,554	**4,653**	5,006
Mean withdrawal	4,044	**6,582**	12,761
Largest withdrawal	5,006	**9,293**	22,126
Panel 4: Female Retiring at Age 65, Portfolio = 35% Stocks, 65% Bonds			
Smallest withdrawal	1,233	**4,648**	5,006
Mean withdrawal	4,097	**5,901**	9,059
Largest withdrawal	5,006	**7,541**	13,303

Source: Congressional Research Service.

For individuals who retire at age 65 or at age 70, average annual withdrawals will be higher than for those who retire at 60 because they will be based on shorter remaining life expectancies. **Table 10** shows the estimated range of withdrawals taken between the ages of 65 and 100 by men and women who retire at age 65 with initial account balances of $100,000. **Table 11** shows the estimated range of withdrawals taken between the ages of 70 and 100 by men and women who retire at age 70 with initial account balances of $100,000.[63]

For a man retiring at age 65 with an initial account balance of $100,000 of which 65% is invested in stocks and 35% is invested in bonds, annual withdrawals could be expected to range from $5,284 to $9,103 with an average withdrawal of $6,861. (See Panel 1 of **Table 10**.) In 5% of the simulations, however, the smallest annual withdrawal was $1,460 or less and in 5% of the simulations the largest withdrawal was $19,513 or more. A woman with the same portfolio retiring at age 65 could expect her annual withdrawals to range from $4,653 to $9,293 with an average withdrawal of $6,582. In 5% of the simulations, the smallest annual withdrawal was $1,554 or less, and in 5% of the simulations, the largest withdrawal was $22,126 or more.

Table 11. Variable Annual Withdrawals Based on Life Expectancy, Retirement at Age 70 (account balance at age 70 = $100,000)

	Annual Withdrawal Based on Remaining Life Expectancy		
	5th Percentile	**Median**	**95th Percentile**
Panel 1: Male Retiring at Age 70, Portfolio = 65% Stocks, 35% Bonds			
Smallest withdrawal	1,412	**6,241**	7,285
Mean withdrawal	4,935	**7,606**	12,127
Largest withdrawal	7,285	**9,552**	17,822
Panel 2: Male Retiring at Age 70, Portfolio = 35% Stocks, 65% Bonds			
Smallest withdrawal	1,230	**6,172**	7,285
Mean withdrawal	5,029	**7,285**	9,694
Largest withdrawal	7,285	**8,511**	12,512
Panel 3: Female Retiring at Age 70, Portfolio = 65% Stocks, 35% Bonds			
Smallest withdrawal	1,519	**5,504**	6,164
Mean withdrawal	4,584	**7,083**	12,239
Largest withdrawal	6,164	**9,282**	19,314
Panel 4: Female Retiring at Age 70, Portfolio = 35% Stocks, 65% Bonds			
Smallest withdrawal	1,273	**5,479**	6,164
Mean withdrawal	4,661	**6,552**	9,365
Largest withdrawal	6,164	**7,978**	12,741

Source: Congressional Research Service.

For a man retiring at age 70 with an initial account balance of $100,000 of which 65% is invested in stocks and 35% is invested in bonds, annual withdrawals could be expected to range from $6,241 to $9,552 with an average withdrawal of $7,606. (See Panel 1 of **Table 11**.) In 5% of the simulations, however, the smallest annual withdrawal was $1,412 or less, and in 5% of the simulations, the largest withdrawal was $17,822 or more. A woman with the same portfolio retiring at age 70, could expect her annual withdrawals to range from $5,504 to $9,282 with an average withdrawal of $7,083. In 5% of the simulations, the smallest annual withdrawal was $1,519 or less, and in 5% of the simulations, the largest withdrawal was $19,314 or more.

SUMMARY OF WITHDRAWAL STRATEGIES: BALANCING RISKS

The uncertainties that retirees face with respect to both life expectancy and annual rates of return on investment make choosing a withdrawal strategy for their retirement accounts one of the most complicated financial decisions of their lives. The decision is even more complicated if retirement assets must be managed over the joint life expectancies of a couple. In light of these complex considerations, some analysts have suggested that "the withdrawal phase of retirement planning may well require more professional guidance and expertise than the accumulation phase."[64]

A retiree who wishes to achieve a predictable annual income can take annual withdrawals that are equal in inflation-adjusted dollars. An individual who chooses a rate of withdrawal that is too high risks spending down the account too quickly, possibly leaving the person impoverished. An individual who chooses a rate of withdrawal that is too low risks spending down the account too slowly, unnecessarily reducing his or her consumption and leaving substantial assets unspent at death. On the other hand, the retiree can choose to take withdrawals that vary from year to year based on the current balance in the account and the retiree's remaining life expectancy. This strategy can result in highly variable annual income.

The results of the analysis that CRS conducted indicate that under certain conditions there is a 95.0% or greater probability a man who retires at age 65 will not fully deplete his retirement account before the earlier of his death or age 90 if his initial withdrawal does not exceed 5.0% of the account balance and if later withdrawals are equal to the first in inflation-adjusted dollars.

Under the same conditions, there is a 95.0% or greater probability that a woman who retires at age 65 will not fully deplete her retirement account before the earlier of her death or age 90 if her initial withdrawal does not exceed 4.5% of the account balance and if later withdrawals are equal to the first in inflation-adjusted dollars. The results hold for both a portfolio invested 65% in stocks and 35% in bonds and for one invested 35% in stocks and 65% in bonds.

The weight that individuals assign to each of the risks they face in retirement will vary from person to person. No one withdrawal strategy will be optimal for everyone. Other researchers have noted that "overall ... there is no clearly dominant strategy, because all involve trade-offs between risk, benefit, and bequest measures, and individual preferences may vary."[65] One way to balance these risks would be to segregate one's retirement funds into two or more accounts and adopt different withdrawal strategies for each. Likewise, one might use some retirement assets to purchase an annuity while taking withdrawals from one or more accounts using one or more withdrawal strategies. Many retirees, however, will not have accumulated enough retirement savings to make these options practical.

APPENDIX A. WHAT IS "MONTE CARLO" ANALYSIS?

Monte Carlo analysis is a method of estimating the probable outcome of an event in which one or more of the variables affecting the outcome are random. The term was coined by mathematicians in the 1940s who likened probability analysis to studying the games of chance played in the casinos of Monte Carlo. One common use of Monte Carlo simulations is to illustrate how the variability of investment rates of return can affect the balances in a retirement account. The essence of a Monte Carlo estimation process is to simulate an event many times, allowing the random variable to vary according to its mathematical mean and variance. Each outcome is then ranked according to the likelihood of its occurrence. Using Monte Carlo methods, analysts can estimate not just the result that will occur "on average," but also the likelihood of results that are significantly above or below the average. In other words, Monte Carlo methods of estimation allow us to incorporate into our estimates the element of *risk*.

Monte Carlo estimation methods utilize not just the average value of a random variable, but also the distribution of values around the average. For example, rates of return in the stock market vary from year to year. The nominal rate of return on the *Standard & Poor's 500* index of stocks averaged 10.3% between 1926 and 2007, but annual rates of return varied widely around this average, producing a standard deviation of 20.0%. Likewise, while the nominal annual return on AAA-rated corporate bonds averaged 6.3% between 1926 and 2007, the standard deviation around this average was 7.0%.

To estimate the likely rate of return that an investment would achieve over a 40-year period, for example, Monte Carlo simulation software generates a rate of return for each year based on the distribution of probable rates of return, as derived from historical data. The program then simulates the 40-year period a second time, again generating a rate of return for each year from the probability distribution of rates of return. The process is repeated until the simulation is completed, and thousands of 40-year investment periods have been simulated. The results of the simulation—in this case, investment rates of return—are then ranked by percentiles. The model CRS used also accounted for the correlation between the rates of return on stocks and bonds and the effects of inflation on real annual returns.

In our simulation of a 40-year period in which 100% percent of assets were invested in common stocks, the mean real rate of return in 10,000 iterations (simulating a 40-year period 10,000 times) was 7.0%, which is the same as the actual mean real rate of return on common stocks in the period from 1926 through 2007. (1.103/1.0305 = 1.70) However, in 5% of those 10,000 iterations, the mean real rate of return over the 40-year period was 1.6% or less, while at the other extreme, in 5% of the 10,000 iterations, the mean real rate of return over the 40-year period was 12.4% or more. In terms of evaluating risk, these results imply an expected annual average real rate of return on common stocks over any given 40-year period of 7.0%, and a 90% probability that the average annual real rate of return over that period will be between 1.6% and 12.4%.

APPENDIX B. UNITED STATES LIFE TABLES, 2004

Table B-1. Life Expectancy at Each Age, in Years

Age	Men	Women
60	20.8	24.0
61	20.0	23.2
62	19.3	22.4

Table B- (Continued)

Age	Men	Women
63	18.5	21.6
64	17.8	20.8
65	17.1	20.0
66	16.4	19.2
67	15.7	18.4
68	15.0	17.7
69	14.4	16.9
70	13.7	16.2
71	13.1	15.5
72	12.5	14.8
73	11.9	14.1
74	11.3	13.5
75	10.7	12.8
76	10.2	12.2
77	9.6	11.5
78	9.1	10.9
79	8.6	10.3
80	8.2	9.8
81	7.7	9.2
82	7.3	8.7
83	6.9	8.2
84	6.5	7.7
85	6.1	7.2
86	5.7	6.8
87	5.4	6.3
88	5.0	5.9
89	4.7	5.6
90	4.4	5.2
91	4.2	4.9
92	3.9	4.5
93	3.7	4.2
94	3.4	3.9
95	3.2	3.7
96	3.0	3.4
97	2.8	3.2
98	2.6	3.0
99	2.5	2.8
100+	2.3	2.6

Source: U.S. Department of Health and Human Services, National Center for Health Statistics, *National Vital Statistics Reports*, vol. 56, no. 9, December 28, 2007, Tables 2 and 3.

Author Contact Information

Janemarie Mulvey
Specialist in Aging Policy
jmulvey@crs.loc.gov, 7-6928

Patrick Purcell
Specialist in Income Security
ppurcell@crs.loc.gov, 7-7571

End Notes

[1] The Bureau of the Census defines the baby boom as people born between 1946 and 1964.

[2] The Social Security Administration estimates that Social Security replaces about 55% of earnings for a career-long low-wage worker, 41% of earnings for a career-long median-wage worker, and 27% of earnings for a career-long high- wage worker.

[3] Life annuities are also sometimes called immediate annuities. This report uses these terms interchangeably.

[4] Some individuals choose not to spend assets because they wish to leave the assets as a bequest to their heirs. However, given that an individual chooses to spend some or all of his or her retirement savings, the relevant question for this analysis is why relatively few choose to do so by purchasing a life annuity.

[5] U.S. National Center for Health Statistics, National Vital Statistics Report, *United States Life Tables, 2004*, Vol. 56(9), (Dec. 2007).

[6] From 1980 to 2007, the Consumer Price Index (CPI) for all goods and services rose from 82.4 to 207.3 while the CPI for medical care rose from 74.9 to 351.1. See Council of Economic Advisers, *Economic Report of the President, February 2008,* Table B-60, p. 295.

[7] See CRS Report RL33364, *The Impact of Medicare Premiums on Social Security Beneficiaries*, by Kathleen Romig,.

[8] CRS estimates based on data reported in CMS Office of the Actuary Memorandum, "Additional Information Regarding Comparisons of Beneficiary Income and Out-of-Pocket Costs For Medicare Supplementary Medical Insurance." March 25, 2008.

[9] Siegel, Jeremy J. *Stocks for the Long-Run.* 2nd ed. New York: McGraw-Hill. 1998.

[10] Johnson, R., et al. "When the Nest Egg Cracks: Financial Consequences of Health Problems, Marital Status Changes, and Job Layoffs at Older Ages," *Urban Institute*, 2006.

[11] Jonathan Skinner, "Are You Sure You're Saving Enough for Retirement?" *Journal of Economic Perspectives*, 21(3), (Summer 2007), p. 59-80.

[12] Hoover, D., S. Crystal, R. Kumar, U. Sambamoorthi, and J. Cantor, "Medical Expenditures During the Last Year of Life: Findings from the 1992-1996 Medicare Current Beneficiary Survey," *Health Services Research*, 37(6), p. 1625- 1642, 2002.

[13] Long-term care refers to a broad range of medical, personal, and supportive services needed by individuals who can no longer care for themselves due to physical or cognitive impairments.

[14] Genworth Financial 2008 Cost of Care Survey, April 2008.

[15] This median income is based on the 99% of households with any income. See CRS Report RL32697, *Income and Poverty Among Older Americans in 2007,* by Patrick Purcell.

[16] The Medicaid statute prohibits individuals from transferring their assets to others in order to qualify for Medicaid. The law also protects some of the income and assets of the community spouse of a nursing home resident so that he or she is not impoverished.

[17] National Association of Variable Annuities, 2007 Factbook.

[18] Although annuity payouts vary depending on the age of retirement, these payouts are not tied to an individual's own life expectancy but rather that of a group of individuals.

[19] Pension Benefit Guaranty Corporation, *Pension Insurance Data Book, 2006.*

[20] Bureau of Labor Statistics, *2007 National Compensation Survey.*

[21] G. Mottola, and S. Utkus, "Lump Sum or Annuity? An Analysis of Choice in DB Pension Payouts," Vanguard Center for Retirement Research, vol. 30, November 2007.

[22] *National Association of Variable Annuities, 2007 Factbook.*

[23] *National Association of Variable Annuities, 2007 Factbook.*

[24] The United States Supreme Court ruled in 1983 that under federal civil rights statutes, employer-sponsored retirement plans cannot offer annuities that differentiate on the basis of gender. See *Arizona Governing Comm. v. Norris*, 463 U.S. 1073 (1983).

[25] *National Association of Variable Annuities, 2007 Factbook.*

[26] Ibid.

[27] *National Association of Variable Annuities, 2007 Factbook.*

[28] The long-term capital gains tax rate, as enacted in the 2003 Jobs and Growth Tax Relief Reconciliation Act, is 15%. Annuity withdrawals are taxed at the marginal tax rate for ordinary income, which could be higher than the capital gains tax rates.

[29] Annuities purchased in the individual market are purchased with after-tax income. The amount of any distribution from an annuity that represents a return to the purchaser of his or her own premium payments is not taxed a second time.

[30] For example, if someone invested $25,000 in a deferred annuity and the value of the annuity when he or she begins to take withdrawals is $50,000, the first $25,000 withdrawn is taxable as ordinary income. The remaining $25,000 is not taxed because it is considered a return of principal to the purchaser.

[31] See IRS Publication 939, *General Rule for Pensions and Ann*uities, Table 5, p 25.

[32] 675 x 12 x 20 = 162,000.

[33] In the IRS tables, the individual's life expectancy at 65 is 20 years, or 240 months. 100,000/240 = 416.

[34] *American Council of Life Insurers*, "Life Insurers' Initiative to Improve the Annuity Sales Environment," Factsheet, February 2008.

[35] Section 17(a) of the Securities Act of 1934, Section 10(b) of the Exchange Act and Rule 10b-5, and Section 206 of the Investment Advisors Act of 1940

[36] See CRS Report RS22974, *Annuities and the Securities and Exchange Commission Proposed Rule 151A*, by Baird Webel.

[37] M. Drinkwater, "Annuitization Study: Profiles and Attitudes," LIMRA International, 2003.

[38] *Best's Review*, "Tis a Gift to be Simple: Complex Annuities Scare Off Both Buyers and Advisers, So the Industry is Offering Less Intimidating Products," April 1, 2006.

[39] Testimony of Minnesota Attorney General Lori Swanson Before the Senate Special Committee on Aging on "Advising Seniors About Their Money: Who is Qualified and Who is Not?" September 5, 2007.

[40] Members of this group include American Council of Life Insurers, National Association of Variable Annuities, National Association of Insurance and Financial Advisors, and the National Association of Independent Life Brokerage Agents.

[41] Mitchell, Olivia, James Poterba, Mark Warshawsky, and Jeffrey Brown, "New Evidence on the Money's Worth of Individual Annuities." *American Economic Review*, 89(5), 1999.

[42] Webb, Anthony. "Is Adverse Selection in the Annuity Market A Big Problem?" Issue Brief, Center for Retirement Research at Boston College, January 2006, Number 40.

[43] See 26 U.S.C. §401(a)(9) and §408(a)(6) and CRS Report RL31770, *Individual Retirement Accounts and 401(k) Plans: Early Withdrawals and Required Distributions*, by Patrick Purcell.

[44] We used the real annual rates of total return on the Standard and Poor's 500 index of common stocks (and its predecessor S& P index) and AAA-rated corporate bonds from 1926 through 2007 to represent the rates of return on investment. The Monte Carlo simulations were performed with Palisade Corporation's @RISK simulation software.

[45] J.J. Spitzer, J.C. Strieter, and S. Singh, "Guidelines for Withdrawal Rates and Portfolio Safety During Retirement," *Journal of Financial Planning*, vol. 20(10), (October 2007).

[46] Spitzer, Strieter, and Singh note that simulations of withdrawal rates of 7.0% or more of the account balance "invariably resulted in unacceptable runout rates."

[47] This is mathematically equivalent to increasing an initial nominal withdrawal by the estimated annual rate of change in the consumer price index. As Spitzer, et al. (2007) note: "Some authors used nominal rates of return and then adjusted the withdrawals each year for inflation such that the withdrawal amount was the same amount in real terms. We chose to use real dollars throughout and avoid the annual inflation adjustment. The outcomes of either process should be the same irrespective of where the adjustment for inflation is made, whether in the withdrawal rate or in the rate of return earned by the investment."

[48] Over the period from 1926 through 2007, the correlation coefficient for the real rates of return on the S&P 500 index and AAA-rated long-term corporate bonds was .236.

[49] In reviewing the literature on retirement account withdrawals, we found that research studies were about evenly divided between those that simulated the effects of fees and taxes and those that did not. Since the purpose of our analysis was to illustrate the effects of rates of withdrawal, rates of return on investment, and life expectancy on account balances, we decided to focus on these variables and ignore fees and taxes.

[50] For these simulations, the initial account balance was assumed to be $100,000; however, the results are independent of the initial balance and apply equally to other amounts.

[51] R.G. Stout and J.B. Mitchell, "Dynamic Retirement Withdrawal Planning, *Financial Services Review*, vol. 15(2), (Summer 2006). The authors further note that, "by incorporating the uncertain retirement life span, [a model of phased withdrawals] generates a more meaningful probability of financial ruin." Stout and Mitchell's analysis looked at one portfolio consisting of 65% stocks and 35% bonds, and their estimates were based on a unisex life expectancy table. CRS tested two portfolios, one of 65% stocks and one of 35% stocks, and we used separate life expectancy tables for men and women.

[52] In each simulation, the individual's probability of having died between age x and age x+1 was compared to a random number generated by the model. If the random number was greater than the probability of having died, the simulation continued for another year. If the random number was lower than the probability of death, the simulation stopped.

[53] Male and female life expectancies at each age were taken from "United States Life Tables, 2004," *National Vital Statistics Reports*, vol. 56(9), U.S. Department of Health and Human Services, Centers for Disease Control and Prevention, National Center for Health Statistics, (December 2007), available at http://www.cdc.gov/nchs/data/nvsr/ nvsr56/nvsr56_09.pdf.

[54] Relatively few people take withdrawals from retirement accounts before age 60 because withdrawals from a traditional IRA or a 401(k) plan taken before age 591/2 are subject to a 10% additional tax except for certain situations defined in law at 26 U.S.C. §72(t). Section 401(a)(9) of the Internal Revenue Code requires owners of traditional IRAs and retired owners of 401(k) plans to start taking distributions after they reach age 70½.

[55] As with the estimates shown in Table 5, for the results presented in Table 6, Table 7, and Table 8, the initial account balance was assumed to be $100,000, but the results are independent of the initial balance and would also apply to other initial account balances.

[56] Most annuities are not adjusted for inflation, and the income therefore declines in value over time.

[57] Ivica Dus, Raimond Maurer, and Olivia Mitchell, "Betting on Death and Capital Markets in Retirement: A Shortfall Risk Analysis of Life Annuities Versus Phased Withdrawal Plans," *Financial Services Review*, vol. 14(3), (Fall 2005).

[58] In this method of withdrawing funds, the fraction withdrawn from the account each year is equal to 1/E(t), where E(t) is the person's remaining years of life expectancy at each age.

[59] Dus, Maurer, and Mitchell, *Financial Services Review*, (2005).

[60] The initial account balance is assumed to be $100,000 only for illustrative purposes. With a smaller initial balance, withdrawals would be smaller, but the relative variability of the withdrawals from year to year would be similar. Data from the Census Bureau indicate that 12.9 million households headed by persons aged 60 or older had a retirement account of some kind at year-end 2005, and that 4.6 million of these households (36%) had account balances of $100,000 or more.

[61] "United States Life Tables, 2004," *National Vital Statistics Reports*, vol. 56(9), (December 2007).

[62] As an example, consider a man age 85 with $25,000 in an account that loses 10% in value each year for three consecutive years. At age 85, he withdraws 1/7.2 (13.9%) of $25,000, or $3,468. One year later, he withdraws 1/6.8 (14.8%) of $19,379 or $2,864. The next year, he withdraws 1/6.3 (15.8%) of $14,864 or $2,343. The following year he withdraws 1/5.9 (16.9%) of $11,269 or $1,896. If the account earns a positive rate of return, the withdrawals could increase or decrease in size, depending on the rate of investment return.

[63] For easier comparison, the initial balance is assumed to be $100,000 in all cases, although an individual who delays retirement until age 65 or 70 might accumulate a larger balance.

[64] Stout and Mitchell, *Financial Services Review*, (2006). Another prominent economist has observed that "retiring employees are ill-equipped to set a sensible drawdown program on their own, especially in the current volatile environment." See the testimony of Shlomo Benartzi, Ph.D. before the House Committee on Education and Labor on October 22, 2008, at http://edlabor.house.gov/testimony/2008-10-22-ShlomoBenartzi.pdf.

[65] Dus, Maurer, and Mitchell, *Financial Services Review*, (2005).

In: Financial Asset Management and Wealth... ISBN: 978-1-60741-696-8
Editor: Terrance G. Waverly

Chapter 3

WILL THE DEMAND FOR ASSETS FALL WHEN THE BABY BOOMERS RETIRE?*

Congressional Budget Office

SUMMARY AND INTRODUCTION

Between 1946 and 1964, some 78 million babies were born in the United States, forming a cohort that has come to be known as the baby-boom generation. When the oldest people in the group turned 62 in 2008, the generation's first members reached the age of eligibility to collect retirement benefits under Social Security and, presumably, began to retire from the workforce. Some economists warn that if the baby- boom generation begins to sell off assets to finance retirement, there could be a steep decline in the demand for assets, particularly stocks (Brooks 2000; Shoven and Schieber 1997; Siegel 1998; Yoo 1994).

The amount of saving by the baby boomers during their working years might already have affected asset markets. Some economists conclude that the increase in baby boomers' demand for assets during their high-saving years explains some of the strength of the stock market over the past two decades (Geanakoplos, Magill, and Quinzii 2004; Lim and Weil 2003). That demand

---

* This is an edited, reformatted and augmented version of a Congressional Budget Office publication dated September 2009.

for assets also could have contributed to the increase in the real (inflation-adjusted) price of housing in the 1970s and 1 980s (Mankiw and Weil 1989), although the sharp rise and fall in house prices during the past decade does not appear to be closely linked to demographic factors.

In principle, if such an unusually large cohort were to sell its accumulated assets to finance consumption during retirement, the total demand for assets in the economy could fall substantially over several decades and the prices of those assets could decline as well. However, empirical evidence about the behavior of earlier groups of retirees suggests that baby boomers will not sell their accumulated assets quickly after they retire. Several factors probably explain that evidence. First, retirees generally are cautious about selling assets to finance consumption, thinking that they might need those assets as they face uncertainty: They might live longer than expected, and medical costs, which are likely to rise as people age, could be higher than anticipated. Second, rather than spend all of their assets, retirees might intentionally retain some to make bequests. Third, wealth in the United States is highly concentrated: About one-third of the nation's financial assets is held by the wealthiest 1 percent of the U.S. population. The wealthiest people do not spend down significant portions of their assets to finance consumption during retirement; in most cases, they die leaving bequests.

Some baby boomers who have lost or spent a significant portion of their retirement assets during the financial turmoil of the past two years might decide to defer retirement, although the empirical evidence is mixed. Such delays could shorten the duration of retirement for those people, reducing the amount of assets they would need to sell off to finance consumption during retirement. The aggregate effect on asset demand might be small, however, if people delayed retiring for only a year or two.

Asset demand also could be affected if retiring baby boomers sell risky assets, such as corporate stocks, in order to shift their portfolios toward safer assets. According to the evidence, however, once they retire, most people do not substantially change the composition of their asset portfolios.

Foreign demand is likely to help sustain the demand for U.S. assets even though some baby boomers might sell some of their assets to finance consumption during retirement. Such an increase in foreign demand is expected to be driven by a rising demand from investors in developing nations with emerging economies and relatively young populations. By contrast, the demand for assets by new immigrants to the United States is unlikely to have much effect on overall demand.

Although the retirement of the baby boomers is not likely to cause a large decline in aggregate demand for assets, several economic studies suggest that the retirement and aging of baby boomers could cause a temporary decrease in asset prices. That prediction of a temporary decrease is based on the studies' theoretical prediction that the retirement of baby boomers will cause the demand for assets to fall more rapidly than the installed stock of capital will be reduced, causing asset prices to fall while the capital stock adjusts. Empirical evidence, however, has not revealed much connection between demographic trends and the changes observed in financial markets.

WHAT DOES SIMPLE THEORY PREDICT ABOUT ASSET DEMAND?

Over the course of most people's working lives, real income tends to peak in late middle age and then to fall as people enter retirement. Economic theory predicts that to smooth spending, people will accumulate assets during their working lives, which they will then sell in retirement to cover living expenses. In the aggregate, then, retirees sell assets to finance their retirement, whereas young and middle-aged workers buy assets to save for old age. As a population ages, the share of older, retired people selling assets increases relative to the share of younger, working people buying them.

Over the next 50 years, the aging of the baby boomers and the smaller cohorts that follow will increase the ratio of older people (those at dissaving ages—at the ages when they might sell off their assets to finance consumption in retirement) to younger people (those at asset-accumulating ages) by 75 percent, potentially generating a significant drop in the demand for assets.

WHAT DOES THE EVIDENCE TELL US?

Although the data generally support the view that people accumulate assets early in life and throughout middle age, some empirical research raises questions about the extent to which people sell their assets rapidly or fully after retirement (for a review, see Hurd 1990).[1] Data from the U.S. Survey of Consumer Finances (SCF), which allow cross-sectional comparisons between people of different ages during particular years, show that household wealth rises sharply when people are in their 40s and 50s but declines gradually as people enter their retirement years (see Figure 1).[2] That pattern is observed both for the mean and for the median value of household net worth.[3]

To be sure, there could be bias in the inferences about a typical age profile that are drawn based on such single-year cross-sections: The data document the behavior of different households of different ages at a single point in time, so the age–wealth profile might simply reflect generational differences in attitudes toward saving; that is, the attitudes toward saving could display a *cohort effect.* However, studies that control for cohort effects display age profiles of asset accumulation that are similar to those discussed here. Those studies also indicate that people dissave very slowly as they reach old age (Poterba 2001, 2004).

Even if the typical individual had an age–wealth profile characterized by significant and fast dissaving after retirement, the aggregate patterns of saving at very old ages would show a much less pronounced drawdown of assets because those patterns are dominated by the behavior of the wealthy. Empirical research indicates that wealthy people live longer than do the poor (see Bernheim 1987) and that they dissave less in old age.

WHY ARE BABY BOOMERS UNLIKELY TO DRAW DOWN ASSETS RAPIDLY IN RETIREMENT?

Several factors suggest that baby-boom retirees, like retirees in earlier groups, are not likely to draw down their assets quickly in retirement. Many will retain their assets as a buffer against high and unanticipated medical expenses and against the risk of outliving their assets. Some will preserve assets to leave as bequests to family members or others. In addition, wealth is distributed unequally among baby boomers. Those with great wealth generally would not spend a substantial portion of their assets to finance the consumption they chose in retirement, whereas the less-well-off would have few assets to liquidate. As a further consideration, although the evidence is mixed, some baby boomers who have lost or spent a significant portion of their retirement assets during the financial turmoil of the past year might decide to defer retirement. Such a response, though, could have a limited effect on the total sales of assets after the baby boomers retire. Finally, empirical evidence also provides little reason to expect that retiring baby boomers will sell risky assets, such as corporate stocks, in order to shift their portfolios toward safer investments.

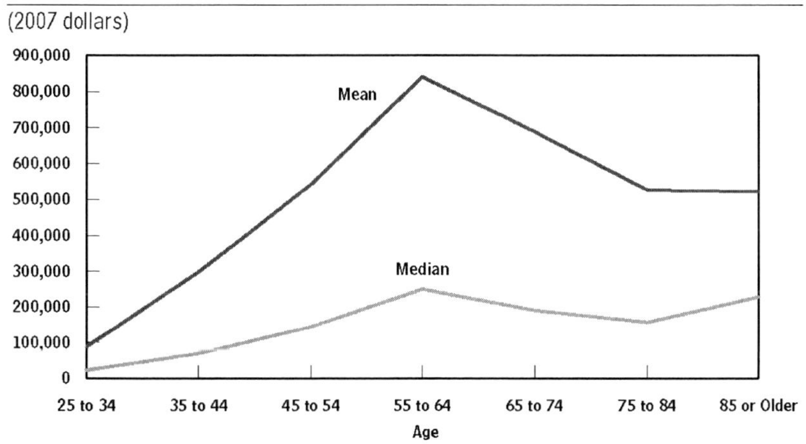

Source: Congressional Budget Office based on Survey of Consumer Finances, 2004.

Note: The median represents the value of the net worth of the bottom 50 percent of the population by total net worth in each age group. The mean is the average value of the net worth within each age group. The distance between the two measures is attributable to the unequal distribution of wealth in the United States.

Data from the 2007 survey show a mean profile that peaks later, in the 65-to-74 age group. The age pattern found in the 2004 data is reported here because that profile is more consistent with previous years of the survey. The profile found in the 2007 data, although more consistent with a general finding that assets decline slowly in old age, is not yet well understood and could be a statistical anomaly.

Figure 1. Net Worth in the United States Over a Lifetime

Saving for Unexpected Events

Like all retirees, baby boomers will have an incentive to spend down their assets slowly in retirement and to keep a buffer of wealth as protection against two particular risks. First, the costs of health care, which are uncertain and tend to increase as people age, point to the importance of retaining assets for out-of-pocket medical expenses. Second, as life expectancy has risen, the variation of life spans also has widened, providing a greater incentive for people to hold some assets in reserve against the risk of an unexpectedly prolonged need to meet living expenses. Both factors suggest the need to draw assets down more slowly in old age than a simple life cycle theory predicts.

The prospect of rising and uncertain out-of-pocket medical expenses can create strong incentives for elderly households to retain their assets, even at later ages. For example, De Nardi, French, and Jones (2006) explained that incorporating rising and uncertain old-age medical expenses into a life cycle model allowed them to closely replicate actual dissaving patterns in old age.[4] In particular, their analysis implies that the median worth of assets for people between the ages of 74 and 81 who are in the fifth quintile of the income distribution is approximately constant at $150,000. That information is consistent with data from the Assets and Health Dynamics Among the Oldest Old (known as the AHEAD survey).[5] Other researchers (Love, Palumbo, and Smith 2008) have confirmed that increasing and uncertain out-of-pocket medical expenditures can help explain the pattern of asset retention in old age.

Dissaving in retirement also tends to proceed slowly because people do not know how long they will live. In theory, someone with an uncertain life span (that is, not knowing when life will end), full health insurance, and no desire to leave a bequest would find it optimal to hold all assets as a lifetime annuity, which would provide income until death, if the annuity could be purchased at a fair premium.[6] If the annuity could not be purchased at a fair premium, there would be an incentive to preserve some wealth to avert the risk of outliving one's assets. Social Security annuities and Medicare reduce that risk by providing a safety net, although for many people those programs offer only partial support for consumption at older ages.[7]

Because private annuities carry high administrative costs and their markets are vulnerable to adverse selection, those markets tend to impose annuity premiums above actuarially fair amounts.[8] As a result, people might forgo private annuities and choose instead to preserve some of their assets even at later ages as a buffer against the possibility of living longer than expected.[9] It is difficult to measure precisely how much people's uncertainty about their life span affects their accumulation of assets, but that effect could be substantial (see Figure 2 and Hubbard, Skinner, and Zeldes 1994). Such uncertainty can significantly reduce the amount by which people draw down assets during retirement.

Saving for Bequests

Baby boomers also would be reluctant to spend down their assets after retirement if they intend to leave a bequest, although the quantitative importance of that factor in explaining the slow rate of dissaving among older people is still not entirely clear.

Several groups of researchers have studied the extent to which bequests are intentional or accidental (that is, occasioned by an early and unexpected death). The distinction is important because if bequests were found to be completely accidental, an intentional bequest motive would not explain the observed tendency for people to dissave slowly in old age. Instead, the observation that people actually do leave bequests would simply reflect what happens when people, by chance, do not end up facing high health costs or living especially long.[10] Establishing that people intend to leave bequests is a necessary first step in elucidating the role of bequests in the observed dissaving patterns of the elderly and wealth dynamics in the United States (De Nardi 2004).

Unfortunately, it is difficult to disentangle bequest motives in the data, so the importance of intentional bequests is still an open issue for research.[11] Some researchers conclude that accidental bequests account for a large share of households' wealth (Abel 1985; Hurd 1987). Others conclude that some significant proportion of bequests are made intentionally (Bernheim, Shleifer, and Summers 1985; De Nardi 2004; Kotlikoff 1988).

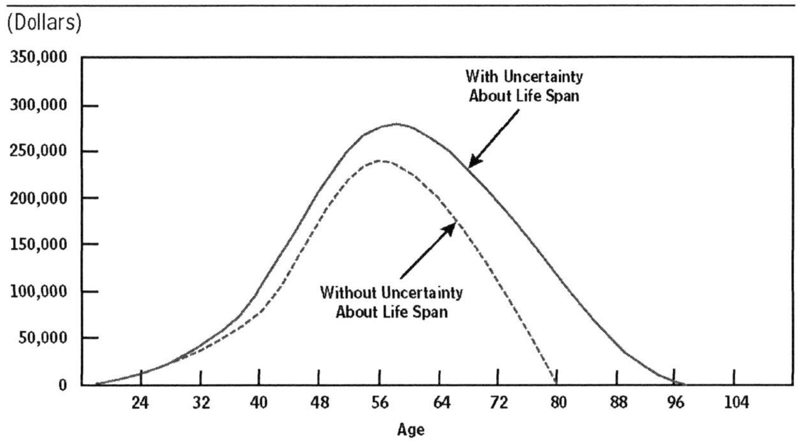

Source: Congressional Budget Office based on Hubbard, Skinner, and Zeldes (1994).
Note: The profile is for an average college graduate; patterns are similar for people in other demographic groups.

Figure 2. Accumulation of Assets, by Age, in a Life Cycle Model

A study by Kopczuk and Lupton (2005) examined whether bequest motives can be identified as intentional or accidental from observed patterns of consumption and saving. The researchers reported that the behavior of about three-quarters of the people in the elderly population indicates an intentional bequest motive and that the average elderly household that exhibits a bequest motive spends about 25 percent less on personal consumption in order to leave a bequest.[12] Those results hold even after the authors controlled for the fact that part of the observed slow rate of spending can be attributed to precautionary savings.[13]

Using different data, from the Health and Retirement Study (HRS) about individuals' intentions to make bequests, Fink and Redaelli (2005) also concluded that a significant number of people exhibit an intentional bequest motive. Those authors reported that about 50 percent of survey respondents indicated a specific intention to leave a bequest and that the strength of the motive correlated with a donor's wealth and social background.[14]

Another study (Ameriks and others 2007) used experimental survey data to disentangle intentional bequest motives from precautionary motives. The survey presented participants with a hypothetical chance to win a $250,000 prize that recipients could divide into a bequest or into spending on a long-term medical care policy. Because most respondents indicated they would devote some portion of the prize to a bequest, the researchers concluded that most respondents had a significant bequest motive.

Regardless of the motives for bequest, some economists have estimated that bequests and other types of transfers made by the elderly account for a significant fraction of people's wealth. The fact that people leave bequests in itself proves that they do not spend down all of their assets in retirement. Brown and Weisbenner (2004) examined SCF data and estimated that total transfers from parents to children in the form of bequests and inter vivos gifts (gifts that are established before the death of the giver) represented between 20 percent and 25 percent of U.S. households' net worth in 1998.[15] The data do not cover charitable transfers of wealth, which implies that inter- generational transfers probably represent an even larger fraction of household wealth than is indicated by those studies.

Unequal Distribution of Assets

Wealth is highly concentrated in the United States. Data from the 2007 SCF indicate that baby-boomer households own more than 50 percent of the value of all outstanding financial assets in the U.S. financial market. The data also show, however, that about one-third of all baby-boomer households own virtually no financial assets (see Figure 3). Even among the two-thirds who do own financial assets, the distribution is particularly concentrated: The wealthiest 10 percent hold more than two- thirds and the wealthiest 1 percent hold almost one-third of all the financial assets held by baby boomers.[16]

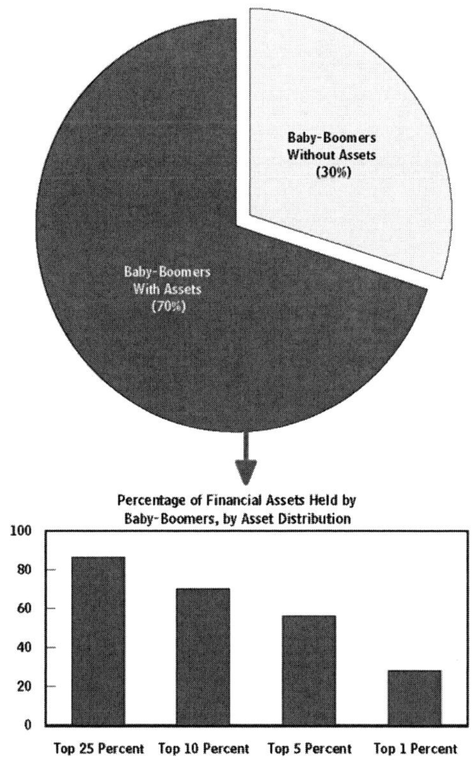

Percentage of the Baby-Boomer Population

Source: Congressional Budget Office.

Note: Financial assets consist of stocks, bonds, mutual funds, individual retirement accounts, and other saving instruments.

Figure 3. Financial Assets Held by Baby-Boomer Households, by Asset Distribution

Such a concentration of wealth can strongly affect the outlook for dissaving after retirement, at the aggregate level, because the wealthiest people do not spend significant portions of their assets during retirement, and the poorest people have no assets to spend. Several economists have shown that the richest people accumulate their wealth at much higher rates relative to their lifetime income than poor people do (for example, see Carroll 2000a, b;

Dynan, Skinner, and Zeldes 2004). Their wealth remains large as they age, showing a low rate of dissaving.[17] To spend down their assets, elderly households must spend more than their income. On average, only 5 percent of elderly people in the top 1 percent of the wealth distribution reported that their spending exceeded their income during the survey years 1992 and 1995 of the SCF (Carroll 2000b). The situation is different for poor households, however, who have nothing to sell in retirement. Thus, the more unequally that wealth is distributed, the less likely it is that baby boomers' retirement will have a significant negative effect on aggregate demand for assets.

Effects of the Financial Turmoil

The financial turmoil of the past year has affected baby boomers in ways that might influence their decisions about spending, retirement, and the rate at which they sell assets after they retire. Most important, the turmoil has reduced the value of many baby boomers' wealth as stock markets crashed and housing prices declined. Additionally, job losses and credit difficulties are likely to have caused some baby boomers to reduce their retirement assets by making early (preretirement) withdrawals from retirement funds.

A sudden loss of retirement wealth is likely to have had the strongest effect on the retirement decisions of baby boomers who are age 55 or older. That age group holds about 60 percent of total retirement account wealth, according to data from the 2007 SCF on the value of assets in retirement accounts, and people in that group will have the shortest time to recover from their losses before retirement.

The decline in retirement wealth can be expected, in theory, to influence the baby boomers' decisions about work, retirement, and consumption expenditures. However, empirical research shows only mixed evidence that the stock market boom of the 1 990s and the subsequent decline of the early 2000s had any effect on the retirement decisions that followed.

One study identified no statistically significant evidence that people postponed retirement (as would be exhibited by an increase in the average age at which people retired) in the aftermath of the stock market decline of 2000 (Coile and Levine 2004). The authors argued that their assessment might reflect the fact that stock holdings, especially direct holdings rather than those in retirement accounts, are concentrated in a relatively small group of people. Even if the market decline of 2000 had influenced retirement decisions made by those people, the group might have been too small to have had much effect on the overall average age of retirement.

Another study that examined survey data indicated that people who held corporate equity immediately before the bull market of the 1990s—either directly or through defined-contribution pension plans—retired, on average, seven months earlier than other respondents did (Coronado and Perozek 2003). Data used in the study signaled that stock market fluctuations might have affected some individual retirement decisions and that those effects might be weaker for people in defined-benefit plans.

Recent shifts in pension coverage toward defined-contribution plans could be expected to increase the influence of stock market fluctuations on retirement behavior. The distribution of equity holdings looks less concentrated if one accounts for assets held through defined-contribution plans and for the fact that such a distribution exposes more people to risk (see Table 1).

Table 1. Distribution of Direct and Indirect Equity Holdings, by Equity-Holding Class

	Bottom				Top	
	50 Percent	60 Percent	80 Percent	90 Percent	5 Percent	1 Percent
Direct	0	0	0.1	3.3	88.9	59.3
Direct and Indirect	0	1.1	8.4	20.0	66.5	38.9

Source: Congressional Budget Office based on the 2007 Survey of Consumer Finances.

Note: Direct equity holdings include stocks owned by baby boomers, directly or through mutual funds. Indirect equity holdings include stocks held through defined-contribution plans, such as individual retirement accounts and 401(k) accounts. Holdings are grouped according to rank in the equity-holding distribution.

Survey data from May 2008 provide some indication about how baby boomers plan to respond to the recent financial turmoil. AARP reported that 60 percent of the baby boomers who were between the ages of 55 and 64 responded that they had already lost value in their retirement assets and other investments.[18] Between 50 percent and 60 percent of the respondents stated that they reacted to the events by reducing unnecessary expenses and postponing major purchases. Thirty-two percent indicated that they intended to respond to the losses by postponing retirement. More than half (56 percent) of survey respondents between the ages of 45 and 54 declared they had already cut major expenses, and 19 percent from that younger group said they expected to postpone retirement. One-fourth of the respondents in both age groups said they had made early withdrawals from their 401(k) retirement plans in the year before the survey.

The baby boomers who decide to delay retirement, perhaps by working into their late 60s or 70s, will not need to draw down their savings as much as they would have if they had retired at a younger age. Additionally, they will have had more time to accumulate savings and they will retire with more Social Security income than they would have received otherwise. Such delays would shorten and therefore reduce their total consumption during retirement, which might reduce the sales of assets necessary to finance that consumption.

Overall, decisions by baby boomers to delay retirement in response to the recent financial turmoil would further slow the rate at which they sell assets to finance retirement. However, any effect of those decisions on the total sales of assets will probably be small if retirements are delayed only by a year or two.

WILL BABY BOOMERS ALTER THE MIX OF ASSETS IN THEIR PORTFOLIOS?

The retirement of the baby-boom generation could influence the relative demand for various types of assets (Campbell 2001). Turmoil in the financial markets might already have affected the portfolio choices of many who are close to retirement. Forty- five percent of respondents between the ages of 55 and 64 in AARP's 2008 market survey said they reduced exposure to risky assets as a consequence of the stock market collapse. It is possible that the rush might have exacerbated market declines in the autumn of 2008 (Carroll 2008).

Empirical evidence, however, suggests that baby boomers are likely to make only slight further changes in their portfolios as they get older. Ameriks and Zeldes (2004) tracked a group of people for several years to identify how their households' portfolios might change as they aged. The data Ameriks and Zeldes used came from TIAA–CREF, a large private pension provider in the United States. When participants in the pension plans enroll, they choose how much to contribute to each investment account, including the amount to invest in the equity accounts; participants are permitted to restructure contributions while they are enrolled. Information on the flows to various accounts can be used to track people's portfolio choices and preferences for risk as they age. The authors reported that more than 50 percent of enrolled households owned no stock. Moreover, households that owned assets did not change their portfolios' allocations very often, and the data show a strong cohort effect on equity holdings. Controlling for that effect, the study shows that most people do not reduce their portfolios' shares of equity when they reach old age and that age is not a significant determinant of changes in asset allocation.[19] That evidence contradicts the existing literature on theory, and most financial planners advise people to change their portfolio allocations over a life cycle to move away from risky assets at old ages.[20]

There also is little evidence that elderly people will draw down housing wealth in retirement. On the basis of data from SCF and HRS, some researchers report that households start accumulating housing wealth early and that home ownership does not decline in old age (Venti and Wise 2001; Yang 2006b). The steady share of housing wealth held by older people could reflect the high transaction costs of trading houses. Moreover, instead of selling, some people who have a large amount of equity choose to keep their homes as potential collateral for loans to meet unanticipated expenses (Yang 2006a).

COULD OTHER FACTORS SUSTAIN THE DEMAND FOR ASSETS?

The discussion so far has concentrated only on the demand for assets by U.S. investors, but demand for assets from foreigners matters as well. In particular, demand for U.S. assets is likely to be sustained by investors from developing and fast-growing countries over the next several decades. In theory, demand for assets also could be sustained by immigrants to the United States, although CBO concludes that immigration is unlikely to have a significant effect.

Demand from Abroad

A rising demand for U.S. financial assets is likely to come from developing countries with emerging economies whose populations are younger or aging less quickly than is the U.S. population. If China and India continue their rapid economic growth, there could be increased demand from those countries for U.S. assets by the time most baby boomers are retired (Siegel 2005).

The population demographics of such developing countries will tend to generate international demand for assets that is diverted toward countries like the United States, which has an older population. Those demographic trends are likely to affect the demand for U.S. assets for decades, but they are expected to disappear sooner for China than for India. The population of India is mostly younger than the U.S. population, and India's population of working-age people who are saving and could potentially demand U.S. assets is expected to grow faster than the corresponding working- age population in the United States. In contrast, China's population is actually aging faster than the U.S. population, but its working-age population is a larger share of its total population and is expected to remain that way at least until 2040. For the next three decades, the fraction of the population that will sell assets to finance retirement is expected to be smaller in China than in the United States (see Table 2).

The potential importance of international demographic trends is highlighted by Fehr, Jokisch, and Kotlikoff (2005), who examined interactions among the United States, Europe (treated in a block as a single country), Japan, and China, and reported that capital flows among countries with different population age structures can help soften the impact of the aging of any particular country's population. The authors posited the effects of projected national demographic changes on the economy of each country. Consideration of China's demographics, in particular, was found to dramatically affect predictions about the asset demand and capital stock that will be available to the United States over the next 40 or 50 years. According to their analysis, through 2050, the effects of demographic trends could be

large enough that the resulting increase in Chinese demand for U.S. assets could more than offset asset sales by baby boomers during their retirement.[21]

Other researchers (Attanasio, Kitao, and Violante 2007; Domeij and Floden 2006; Henriksen 2002) have taken a similar approach and reported that demographic trends can be expected to have a substantial effect on international flows of capital. Their studies demonstrate that, when different regions or countries have populations that exhibit different demographic patterns, international capital flows can mitigate the macroeconomic effects of demographic transitions that occur within any particular region or country.

Table 2. Population Projections for the United States, India, and China

	2000	2010	2020	2030	2040	2050
Fertility Rate[a]						
United States	2.1	2.1	2.0	2.0	1.9	1.9
India	3.4	2.8	2.3	2.0	1.9	1.9
China	1.3	1.4	1.5	1.7	1.8	1.9
Life Expectancy at Birth (Years)						
United States	77.1	78.3	79.1	79.9	81.0	81.6
India	61.5	64.9	68.5	71.4	73.8	75.9
China	71.5	72.6	73.8	75.3	77.1	78.7
Age Distribution						
Percentage of Population Under Age 15						
United States	21.8	20.5	20.0	19.3	18.5	17.9
India	34.1	29.9	26.3	22.6	19.7	18.3
China	24.8	19.5	18.4	16.9	15.6	15.7
Percentage of Population, Ages 15 to 64						
United States	65.9	66.6	64.1	61.5	61.7	62.1
India	61.0	64.4	66.7	68.1	68.3	66.8
China	68.4	72.2	69.7	66.8	62.1	60.7
Percentage of Population, Ages 65 to 90						
United States	12.3	12.8	15.9	19.2	19.8	20.0
India	4.9	5.7	7.0	9.3	12.0	14.8
China	6.8	8.3	11.9	16.3	22.3	23.6

Source: United Nations population database for 2003 and 2005, medium variant projections.

a. Fertility rate is the number of children per woman.

Brooks (2003) found that the actual differences in population trends around the world are likely to have been an important determinant of international capital flows. For example, such population trends can explain an inflow of capital in past decades from the European Union and Japan (where aging populations were at the peak years of saving for retirement) toward countries like the United States (where corresponding aging of the population and its effect on net saving for retirement were relatively less pronounced). Brooks also suggests that the aging of the baby boomers can be expected to cause capital to flow out of the United States toward countries with younger populations and faster growing economies during the peak years when baby boomers are expected to save for retirement. Similarly, in reverse, those patterns of saving and population aging can be expected to cause an inflow of capital to the United States by 2020, when, Brooks asserts, most of the baby boomers will be dissaving to finance retirement.

Ludwig, Krueger, and Boersch-Supan (2007) predicted that baby-boomer retirements between 2020 and 2030 could cause a decline in the current account balance in the United States equal to almost 2 percent of gross domestic product.

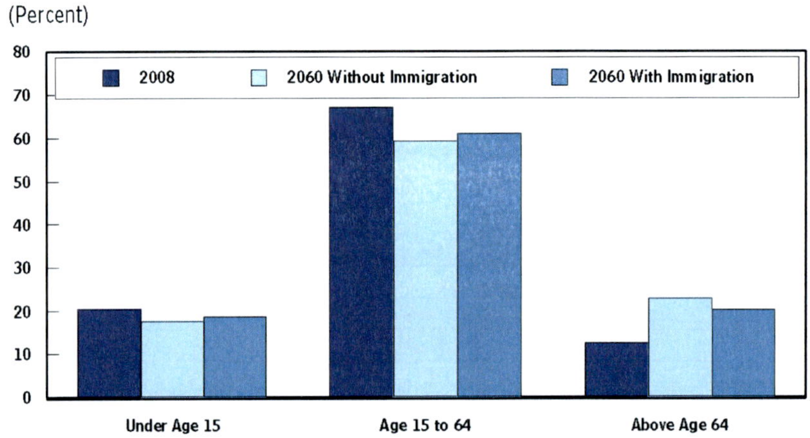

Source:Congressional Budget Office.

Note:CBO's long-term microsimulation model incorporates the methodology for projecting net immigration that was adopted by the Social Security Administration's Office of the Chief Actuary and reported in its *2008 Trustees Report on Social Security*.

Figure 4. Effect of Immigration on the Distribution of the U.S. Population, by Age, 2008 and 2060

Demand Among Immigrants

In principle, immigration also could help sustain the demand for U.S. assets after the baby boomers retire. However, if immigration continues at the current rate, it is not likely to have much effect on the age structure of the U.S. population or on the potential demand for U.S. assets.

Currently, an estimated 1.6 million legal and undocumented immigrants settle each year in the United States; about 350,000 people emigrate, resulting in net annual immigration of 1.25 million people.[22] Immigration will be a major source of growth in the U.S. population, but it will only marginally slow the general aging of the U.S. population (see Figure 4).[23] In 2060, immigration will have little effect on the working-age share of the population—the group that demands assets. Accounting for immigration, the working-age share will constitute 61 percent of the popula-tion in 2060—almost the same as the working-age share without immigration (59.3 percent). Immigration will contribute somewhat more to decreasing the pro-portion of the population that is elderly—the group that sells assets. Accounting for immigration, the elderly share will be 20.2 percent in 2060; without immigration, the elderly share will be 22.8 percent. Although immigration is projected to reduce what is called the age–dependency ratio (the number of people over age 64 divided by the number between 15 and 64), at current rates over the next 50 years, immigration will have little effect on the expected sharp increase in the share of the population constituted by the elderly (see Figure 5 and Figure 6).

Immigrants typically exhibit higher fertility rates than do people who were born in the United States. Thus, immigration contributes to an increase in the share of the population at the other end of the age spectrum—those who are under the age of 15.[24] Immigrant households typically have more dependents and are likely to dedicate more resources to child rearing. Their income profiles also appear different from those of U.S. natives, especially during the first few years after arriving in the United States (for example, immigrants who entered between 1990 and 2000, see Figure 6).

Despite a measurable and significant presence at the high end of the income distribution, immigrants are still more concentrated in lower-income groups than are U.S. natives—a phenomenon that is more pronounced among the most recent arrivals to the United States. Duleep and Dowhan (2008) reported that although immigrants generally earn far less than natives do when they enter the United States and their income grows significantly after about 10 years in the country, catching up with natives is never fully accomplished. Long periods of transition in the income profiles and the higher number of dependents relative to natives add more reasons to the pure demographic figures mentioned above to conclude that immigration will contribute little to national savings.

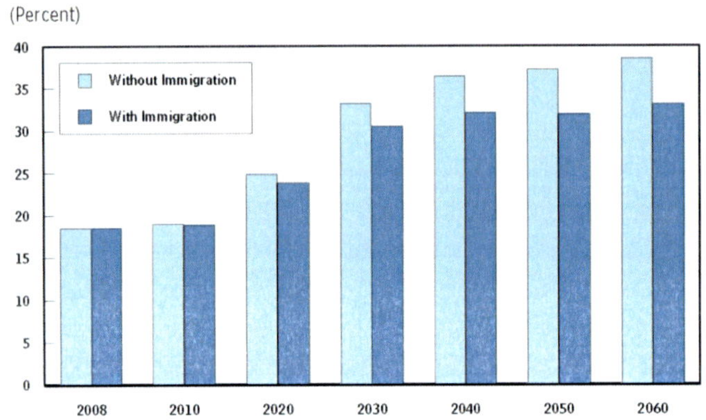

Source: Congressional Budget Office.

Note: The age–dependency ratio expresses the number of people age 65 and older (who often are not in the labor force) divided by the number of people between the ages of 15 and 64 (who are more likely to be in the labor force).

Figure 5. The Age–Dependency Ratio for the United States, With and Without Immigration, 2008 to 2060

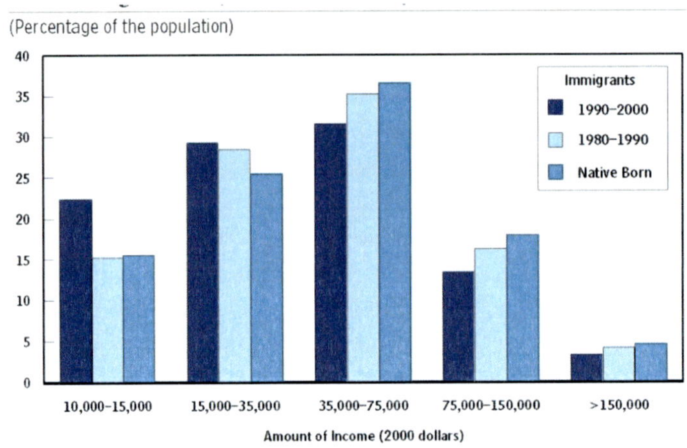

Source: Congressional Budget Office based on the 2000 Current Population Survey, U.S. Census Bureau.

Figure 6. Income Distribution for the Native Born and for U.S. Immigrants, by Period of Entry

EFFECT ON ASSET PRICES

Several economic studies have predicted that the aging and retirement of the baby boomers will dramatically reduce asset prices and rates of return (Siegel 1998; Shoven and Schieber 1997).[25] Those studies are based on an unproven premise that the retirement of such a relatively large cohort will create a dramatic drop in the demand for assets. The simplest analysis assumes that the stock of installed capital is fixed and that asset prices will fall because the demand for assets by younger cohorts will not be enough to offset the fall in demand by retiring cohorts. If that simple analysis told the whole story, asset prices would fall significantly as baby boomers retired and sold their assets. As discussed previously, however, the baby boomers' demand for assets and savings probably will not fall quickly, so any corresponding decline in the price of assets is likely to be similarly muted.

More comprehensive analysis (Abel 2001, 2003; Brooks 2002) accounts for the fact that the retirement of baby boomers also will contribute to reduced growth in the economy's labor supply, and it further recognizes that the stock of installed capital can change.[26] Even with those additional considerations, the more comprehensive analysis suggests that the baby boomers' retirement will cause the prices of real assets to be temporarily lower than if the demographic shift had not occurred.[27] As baby boomers retire, their exit from the labor force will not be fully offset by the entry of workers from younger cohorts, thus contributing to an increase in the capital intensity of production (the amount of capital per worker).[28] Capital intensity will increase temporarily to the extent that the capital stock does not adjust as quickly as the change in labor supply. A transitory increase in capital intensity would lead to a temporary increase in real wages and a temporary decrease in the return on capital.[29]

The size of the capital adjustment, the time it takes to occur, and its effect on real asset prices and the return on capital will depend on several factors. For reasons discussed earlier in this paper, people do not spend their accumulated wealth quickly or fully after they retire. Such a life cycle pattern of spending suggests that downward adjustment in the demand for assets will be gradual and limited. Investment frictions and capital market imperfections also are likely to slow the rate at which the capital stock is reduced. The price of installed capital could fall temporarily if the capital stock is reduced more slowly than the demand for assets declines.[30]

In addition to those expected patterns of change in the real economy, the prices of financial assets also depend on evaluations by participants in the financial markets. Retrospective examination of financial market data does not support a prediction that the retirement of baby boomers will cause financial asset prices to fall noticeably. Brooks (2006) studied a historical time series of stock and bond prices for most of the developed economies to investigate whether it is possible to establish empirically that countries that are characterized by aging populations experience reductions in financial price indices. His results did not establish much of a connection between such demographic trends and changes observed in financial markets.

REFERENCES

Abel, Andrew B. (1985). "Precautionary Saving & Accidental Bequests." *American Economic Review,* vol. *75*, no. 4 (September), pp. 777–791.

———. 2001. "Will Bequests Attenuate the Predicted Meltdown in Stock Prices When Baby Boomers Retire?" *Review of Economics and Statistics,* vol. *83*, no. 4 (November), pp. 589–595.

———. 2003. "The Effects of a Baby Boom on Stock Prices and Capital Accumulation in the Presence of Social Security." *Econometrica,* vol. *71*, no. 2 (March), pp. 55 1–578.

Ameriks, John, & Stephen P. Zeldes. (2004). "How Do Household Portfolio Shares Vary with Age?" Unpublished manuscript. www.ifk-cfs.de/papers/rtn0505_paper_Ameriks_ Zeldes.pdf.

Ameriks, John, & others. (2007). *The Joy of Giving or Assisted Living? Using Strategic Surveys to Separate Bequest and Precautionary Motives.* Working Paper 13105. Cambridge, Mass.: National Bureau of Economic Research. May. www.nber.org/papers/w13105.pdf.

Attanasio, Orazio, Sagiri Kitao, & Giovanni L. Violante. (2007). "Global Demographic Trends and Social Security Reform." *Journal of Monetary Economics,* vol. *54*, no. 1 (January), pp. 144–198.

Bernheim, B. Douglas. (1987). "Dissaving After Retirement: Testing the Pure Life Cycle Hypothesis." In *Issues in Pension Economics*. Zvi Bodie, John B. Shoven, and David A. Wise, eds. Chicago: University of Chicago Press, Chapter 9. www.nber.org/chapters/ c6861 .pdf.

Bernheim, B. Douglas, Andrei Shleifer, & Lawrence H. Summers. (1985). "The Strategic Bequest Motive." *Journal of Political Economy*, vol. *93*, no. 6 (December), pp. 1045–1076.

Brooks, Robin. 2000. *What Will Happen to Financial Markets When the Baby Boomers Retire?* International Monetary Fund Working Paper WP/00/18. February. www.imf.org/ external/pubs/ft/wp/2000/wp0018. pdf.

———. 2002. "Asset-Market Effects of the Baby Boom and Social-Security Reform." *American Economic Review: Papers & Proceedings,* vol. *92*, no. 2 (May), pp. 402–406.

———. 2003. "Population Aging and Global Capital Flows in a Parallel Universe." *IMF Staff Papers,* vol. *50*, no. 2, pp. 200–221. www.imf.org/External/Pubs/FT/staffp/2003/02/pdf/ brooks.pdf.

———. 2006. "Demographic Change and Asset Prices." Manuscript prepared for the Demography and Financial Markets Conference (July 23–25) organized by the Reserve Bank of Australia. www.rba.gov.au/PublicationsAndResearch/Conferences/2006/Brooks.pdf.

Brown, Jeffrey R. (2007). *Rational and Behavioral Perspectives on the Role of Annuities in Retirement Planning.* Working Paper 13537. Cambridge, Mass.: National Bureau of Economic Research. October. www.nber.org/papers/w13537.pdf.

Brown, Jeffrey R. & Scott J. Weisbenner. (2004). "Intergenerational Transfers and Savings Behavior." In *Perspectives on the Economics of Aging.* David A. Wise, ed. Chicago: University of Chicago Press.

Brown, Jeffrey R., & others. (2008). "Why Don't People Insure Late-Life Consumption? A Framing Explanation of the Under-Annuitization Puzzle." *American Economic Review: Papers & Proceedings,* vol. *98*, no. 2 (May), pp. 304–309.

Campbell, John Y. 2001. "A Comment on James M. Poterba's 'Demographic Structure and Asset Returns.'" *Review of Economics and Statistics,* vol. *83*, no. 4 (November), pp. 585–588.

Carroll, Christopher D. (2000a). *Portfolios of the Rich.* Working Paper 7826. Cambridge, Mass.: National Bureau of Economic Research. August. www.nber.org/papers/w7826.pdf.

———. (2000b). "Why Do the Rich Save So Much?" Unpublished manuscript. www.econ.jhu.edu/people/ccarroll/Why.pdf.

———. 2008. "*Scary Story: Global Stock Declines and the Baby Boom.*" FT.com. October 13. http://blogs.ft.com/wolfforum/2008/10/are-global-stock-declines-a-babyboom-bust/.

Choi, James J., & others. (2004). "For Better or For Worse: Default Effects and 401(k) Savings Behavior." In *Perspectives on the Economics of Aging*. David Wise, ed. Chicago: University of Chicago Press.

Coile, Courtney C., & Phillip B. Levine. (2004). *Bulls, Bears, and Retirement Behavior.* Working Paper 10779. Cambridge, Mass.: National Bureau of Economic Research. September. www.nber.org/papers/w10779.pdf.

Congressional Budget Office. (2008). *Updated Long-Term Projections for Social Security.* August.

Coronado, Julia Lynn, & Maria Perozek. (2003). *Wealth Effects and the Consumption of Leisure: Retirement Decisions During the Stock Market Boom of the 1900s.* Finance and Economics Discussion Series 2003-20. Board of Governors of the Federal Reserve System. May (updated June 4, 2003). www.federalreserve.gov/pubs/feds/2003/200320/ 200320pap.pdf.

Davidoff, Thomas, Jeffrey Brown, & Peter Diamond. 2003. *Annuities and Individual Welfare.* CRR WP 2003-11. Chestnut Hill, Mass.: Center for Retirement Research at Boston College. May. http://crr.bc.edu/images/stories/Working_Papers/wp_2003-11.pdf? phpMyAdmin=43ac483c4de9t5 1d9eb4 1.

De Nardi, Mariacristina. (2004). "Wealth Inequality and Intergenerational Links." *Review of Economic Studies*, vol. *71*, no. 3 (July), pp. 743–768.

De Nardi, Mariacristina, Eric French, & John Bailey Jones. (2006). *Differential Mortality,Uncertain Medical Expenses, and the Saving of Elderly Singles.* Working Paper 2005-13. Federal Reserve Bank of Chicago. September 14. www.chicagofed.org/publications/ workingpapers/wp2005_1 3.pdf.

Domeij, David, & Martin Floden. (2006). "Population Aging and International Capital Flows." *International Economic Review,* vol. *47*, no. 3, pp. 1013–1032.

Duleep, Harriet Orcutt, & Daniel J. Dowhan. (2008). "Research on Immigrant Earnings." *Social Security Bulletin,* vol. *68*, no. 1, pp. 31–50. www.ssa.gov/policy/docs/ssb/v68n1/ 68n1p31.pdf.

Dynan, Karen E., Jonathan Skinner, & Stephen P. Zeldes. (2004). "Do the Rich Save More?" *Journal of Political Economy*, vol. *112*, no. 2 (April), pp. 397–444.

Fehr, Hans, Sabine Jokisch, & Laurence J. Kotlikoff. (2005). *Will China Eat Our Lunch or Take Us Out to Dinner? Simulating the Transition Paths of the U.S., EU, Japan, and China.*Working Paper 11668. Cambridge, Mass.: National Bureau of Economic Research. September. www.nber.org/papers/w11668.pdf.

Fink, Günther, & Silvia Redaelli. (2005). *Understanding Bequest Motives—An EmpiricalAnalysis of Intergenerational Transfers.* Working Paper 42/2005. Amsterdam: De Nederlandsche Bank. May. www.dnb.nl/en/binaries/ Working%20Paper%20No.%2042-2005_tcm47-146699.pdf.

Finkelstein, Amy. (2003). "Comment on 'Impact of Defined Contribution Plans.'" In *Death and Dollars: The Role of Gifts and Bequests in America.* Alicia H. Munnell and Annika Sunden, eds. Washington, D.C.: Brookings Institution Press, pp. 307–316.

Finkelstein, Amy, & James Poterba. (2004). "Adverse Selection in Insurance Markets: Policyholder Evidence from the U.K. Annuity Market." *Journal of Political Economy,* vol. *112,* no. 1 (February), pp. 183–208. www.journals.uchicago.edu/doi/pdf/10.1086/ 379936.

Geanakoplos, John, Michael Magill, & Martine Quinzii. (2004). *Demography and the Long- Run Predictability of the Stock Market.* Cowles Foundation Discussion Paper 1380R. New Haven, Conn.: Cowles Foundation for Research in Economics, Yale University. April. http://cowles.econ.yale.edu/P/cd/d13b/d1380-r.pdf.

Henriksen, E. R., (2002). "*A Demographic Explanation of U.S. and Japanese Current Account Behavior.*" Unpublished manuscript. Pittsburgh, Pa.: Carnegie Mellon University.

Hubbard, R. Glenn, Jonathan Skinner, & Stephen P. Zeldes. (1994). "The Importance of Precautionary Motives in Explaining Individual and Aggregate Saving." *Carnegie– Rochester Conference Series on Public Policy,* vol. *40,* no. 1 (June), pp. 59–125.

Hurd, Michael D. (1987). "Savings of the Elderly and Desired Bequests." *American Economic Review,* vol. *77,* no. 3 (June), pp. 298–3 12.

———. 1990. "Research on the Elderly: Economic Status, Retirement, and Consumption and Saving." *Journal of Economic Literature,* vol. *28,* no. 2 (June), pp. 565–637.

Hurd, Michael D., James P. Smith, & Julie Zissimopoulos. (2007). *Inter- Vi vos Giving Over the Lifecycle.* RAND Working Paper WR-524. Santa Monica, Calif.: RAND Corporation. October. www.rand.org/pubs/ working_ papers/2007/RAND_WR524.pdf.

Jagannathan, Ravi, & Narayana R. Kocherlakota. (1996). "Why Should Older People Invest Less in Stocks Than Younger People?" *Federal Reserve Bank of Minneapolis Quarterly Review,* vol. *20,* no. 3 (Summer), 1996, pp. 11–23.

Khan, Aubhik, & Julia Thomas. (2008). "Adjustment Costs." In *The New Palgrave Dictionary of Economics,* 2nd ed. Stephen N. Durlaf and Lawrence E. Blume, eds. New York: Palgrave Macmillan. www.dictionaryofeconomics.com/article?id=pde2008_N000151&q =Adjustment%20costs&topicid=&result_number= 1#citations.

Kopczuk, Wojciech, & Joseph P. Lupton. (2005). *To Leave or Not to Leave: The Distribution of Bequest Motives.* Working Paper 11767. Cambridge, Mass.: National Bureau of Economic Research. November. www.nber.org/papers/w11767.pdf.

Kotlikoff, Laurence J. (1988). "Intergenerational Transfers and Savings." *Journal of Economic Perspectives,* vol. 2, no. 2, pp. 41–58.

Lim, Kyung-Mook, and David N. Weil. (2003). "The Baby Boom and the Stock Market Boom." *Scandinavian Journal of Economics,* vol. *105*, no. 3 (September), pp. 359–378.

Love, David A., Michael G. Palumbo, & Paul A. Smith. (2008). *The Trajectory of Wealth in Retirement.* Finance and Economics Discussion Series 2008-13. Board of Governors of the Federal Reserve System. www.federalreserve.gov/Pubs/feds/2008/200813/20081 3pap.pdf.

Ludwig, Alexander, Dirk Krueger, & *Factor Prices, International Capital Flows, and Their Differential Effects on the Welfare of Generations.* Working Paper 13185. Cambridge, Mass.: National Bureau of Economic Research. June. www.nber.org/papers/w13185.pdf?new_window=1.

Madrian, Brigitte C., and Dennis F. Shea. (2001). "The Power of Suggestion: Inertia in 401(k) Participation and Savings Behavior." *Quarterly Journal of Economics,* vol. *116*, no. 4 (November), pp. 1149–1 187.

Mankiw, N. Gregory, & David N. Weil. (1989). "The Baby Boom, the Baby Bust, and the Housing Market." *Regional Science and Urban Economics,* vol. *19*, no. 2 (May), pp. 235–258.

Merton, Robert C. (1971). "Optimum Consumption and Portfolio Rules in a Continuous-Time Model." *Journal of Economic Theory,* vol. *3*, no. 4 (December), pp. 373–413.

Poterba, James M. (2001). "Demographic Structure and Asset Returns." *Review of Economics and Statistics,* vol. 83, no. 4 (November), pp. 565–584.

———. 2004. *The Impact of Population Aging on Financial Markets.* Working Paper 10851. Cambridge, Mass.: National Bureau of Economic Research. October. www.nber.org/ papers/w10851 .pdf.

Poterba, James M., and Andrew A. Samwick. 1997. *Household Portfolio Allocation Over the Life Cycle*. Working Paper 6185. Cambridge, Mass.:

National Bureau of Economic Research. www.nber.org/papers/w6185.pdf?new_window=1.

Shoven, John B., & Sylvester J. Schieber. (1997). *The Aging of the Baby Boom Generation: The Impact on Private Pensions, National Saving, and Financial Markets.* Working Paper. Washington, D.C.: American Council for Capital Formation, Center for Policy Research. February. www.accf.org/publications.php?pubID=21.

Siegel, Jeremy J. 1998. *Stocks for the Long Run.* New York: McGraw-Hill.

———. 2005. *The Future for Investors: Why the Tried and the True Triumph Over the Bold and the New.* New York: Crown Business.

Social Security Administration. (2008). *The 2008 Annual Report of the Board of Trustees of the Federal Old-Age and Survivors Insurance and Federal Disability Insurance Trust Funds.* April 10. www.ssa.gov/OACT/TR/TR08/tr08.pdf.

Venti, Steven F., & David A. Wise. (2001). *Aging and Housing Equity: Another Look.* Working Paper 8608. Cambridge, Mass.: National Bureau of Economic Research. November. www.nber.org/papers/w8608.pdf.

Yaari, Menahem E. (1965). "Uncertain Lifetime, Life Insurance, and the Theory of the Consumer." *Review of Economic Studies,* vol. *32*, no. 2 (April), pp. 137–150.

Yang, Fang. (2006a). *Consumption Over the Life Cycle: How Different Is Housing?* Working Paper 635. Research Department, Federal Reserve Bank of Minneapolis. August. www.minneapolisfed.org/research/WP/WP635.pdf.

———. (2006b). "How Do Household Portfolios Vary with Age?" Unpublished manuscript.

Yoo, Peter S. (1994). *Age Dependent Portfolio and Selection.* Working Paper 1994-003A. Federal Reserve Bank of St. Louis. February. http://research.stlouisfed.org/wp/1994/94-003.pdf.

End Notes

[1] Even abstracting from such research about the dissaving behavior of the elderly, the fact that people die leaving large bequests shows directly that many retirees do not dissave fully in retirement.

[2] Data on net worth do not include assets people hold indirectly through defined-benefit pension plans, which also sell retirees' assets to pay out pension benefits (see Shoven and Schieber 1997). However, the prevalence of defined-benefit plans has declined significantly over the past several decades, and that decline is expected to continue.

[3] Mean net worth is an arithmetic average of household net worth. The median is the point in a distribution at which half of the observations have higher and half have lower net worth. The difference between the mean and the median stems from the nation's pronounced concentration of wealth in a relatively small segment of the population.

[4] The life cycle model they study also accounts for uncertain life spans.

[5] The AHEAD survey studies a subsample of people ages 70 and older who participate in the Health and Retirement Study, a national longitudinal study of the economic, health, marital, and family status of older people conducted by the University of Michigan under the sponsorship of the National Institute of Aging.

[6] Such a premium is technically defined as "actuarially fair," and the additional costs of becoming insured are called transaction costs (Davidoff, Brown, and Diamond 2003; Yaari 1965).

[7] For some people, Social Security and Medicare provide only incomplete insurance against the risk of not being able to finance consumption if one outlives his or her own wealth.

[8] Adverse selection occurs when people with short expected life spans choose not to purchase annuities, causing higher premiums for people who remain in the pool. Several researchers have examined the phenomenon in the annuity markets (see, for example, Brown and others 2008; Finkelstein and Poterba 2004). For a literature review, see Brown (2007).

[9] Premiums for individual annuities totaled $30 billion in 2007; the potential market is estimated at more than $200 billion. Data on the total market sales of annuities are estimated by Beacon Research and are available online by product type; see www.primenewswire.com/newsroom/ news.html?d= 126723.

[10] See Finkelstein (2003) for a discussion of the importance of distinguishing between intentional and accidental bequests.

[11] This point is highlighted by Finkelstein (2003).

[12] Kopczuk and Lupton (2005) used data from the AHEAD survey. To overcome limitations of earlier studies, the authors did not assume that parents are the only people who can have an intentional bequest motive.

[13] The sensitivity analysis that Kopczuk and Lupton performed might not be sufficiently rigorous, however. Their conclusions depend fundamentally on just a single variable that was constructed from questions about survey respondents' expectations about future out-of-pocket medical expenditures.

[14] Fink and Redaelli's assessments should be interpreted cautiously because they assumed that survey respondents who indicated that they expected to leave a bequest with 100 percent likelihood would signal that they intentionally saved to do so. But respondents' reported expectations might also signal a belief they had saved enough as a precaution against outliving their wealth and that they did not expect to exhaust their assets before death.

[15] Hurd, Smith, and Zissimopuolos (2007) examined HRS longitudinal data from 1992 to 2002 and concluded that the amount of cash couples give to children dramatically increases when the givers reach the age of 80. The implication could be that many parents prefer to make bequests in the form of gifts at very old ages. As part of their tax-planning strategy, couples who are wealthy enough to be potentially subject to the estate tax if they leave bequests might prefer instead to make inter vivos gifts.

[16] Financial assets include stocks, bonds, mutual funds, individual retirement accounts, and other retirement saving instruments. Measures of wealth that include real assets, such as housing, would feature a less uneven distribution in the U.S. population. This paper focuses in particular on financial assets because they are considered liquid assets and some economists have shown that retirees do not decrease their housing stock even at old ages (see Yang 2006b).

[17] Wealthy people do not necessarily draw down all their assets to finance consumption in retirement because they tend to accumulate wealth for reasons other than simply to smooth consumption over a lifetime. Carroll (2000a) asserts that wealthy people save in a way that

does not conform to a simple life cycle model and suggests that their behavior could be explained, for example, by strong bequest motives.

[18] The report, "The Economic Slowdown's Impact on Middle-Aged and Older Americans," http://assets.aarp.org/rgcenter/econ/economy_survey.pdf, is cited here for its qualitative assessment of the effects on baby boomers' decisionmaking that are attributable to recent conditions in the financial markets.

[19] Other studies have exhibited strong evidence of such inertia in portfolio allocation as people age (see Choi and others 2004; Madrian and Shea 2001; and Poterba and Samwick 1997).

[20] See, for example, the seminal theoretical work by Merton (1971) and by Jagannathan and Kocherlakota (1996).

[21] Fehr and coauthors' results depend not only on demographic patterns. Those patterns are not the only factor that can be expected to influence aggregate savings in China. China's high rates of saving and growth and its fiscal policies are currently very different from those at work in the United States and other more developed countries. The results depended on several strong assumptions (in addition to the demographic patterns): that successive cohorts of Chinese people will continue to save the way current cohorts do, that the Chinese government will continue its current policy of restrained growth in expenditures, and that Chinese technology will catch up with that in the United States.

[22] See Center for Immigration Studies, www.cis.org/impact_on_population.html.

[23] This conclusion is based on CBO's projections from its long-term microsimulation model (Congressional Budget Office 2008). Immigration might ultimately reduce the aging of the U.S. population if future immigration rates are substantially greater than CBO projects.

[24] The age of 15 is used for compatibility with international data shown in Table 2 on page 14.

[25] This discussion refers to assets as the total claims to capital installed in the companies. The prices of assets that promise the payment of a fixed payout, such as Treasury bonds, move in the opposite direction from the rates of return. The price of an asset can change in the same direction as the rate of return when the payout stream also is variable, as it is for the assets discussed in this analysis.

[26] Long-term demographic trends other than the aging and retirement of the baby-boom generation will drive down the long-term rate of growth in the labor supply.

[27] Abel (2001), however, warns that it is difficult to draw firm conclusions about the effect on the prices of assets.

[28] The labor force is likely to grow more slowly as a result of the general aging of the population, not just of baby boomers (Social Security Administration 2008).

[29] Eventually, changes in saving and investment decisions in response to the lower return can be expected to cause the capital stock to adjust and the capital intensity to fall back in the direction of, but not all the way to, its previous level.

[30] Economic literature usually refers to this as the Tobin's q or the shadow price of installed capital relative to consumption goods. For a comprehensive dissertation on investment adjustment frictions, see Khan and Thomas (2008).

INDEX

accounting, 17, 42
adjustment, 10, 28, 43, 54, 59, 95, 115, 123
advertisements, 70
advertising, 71, 73
aggregate demand, 99, 106
aging population, 112, 116
algorithm, 53
annual rate, 60, 66, 75, 78, 88, 90, 95
arithmetic, 122
assessment, 74, 107, 123
asset demand, 98, 110
assumptions, 11, 33, 34, 43, 46, 52, 79, 123
attitudes, 100
Attorney General, 95
authors, 51, 95, 104, 107, 109, 110, 122
Baby Boom Generation, 39, 121
baby boomers, vii, viii, 1, 97, 98, 99, 100, 101, 105, 106, 107, 108, 109, 110, 111, 112, 113, 115, 116, 123
background, 104
base year, 29
behavior, vii, 1, 2, 3, 5, 15, 29, 49, 52, 98, 100, 104, 107, 121, 123
bias, 5, 19, 23, 52, 100
bonds, 7, 60, 65, 75, 76, 77, 78, 79, 86, 87, 88, 89, 90, 95, 105, 122, 123
borrowing, 52
breakdown, 8
buffer, 4, 35, 100, 101, 102
buyer, 73
capital flows, 110, 111, 112
capital gains, 3, 16, 28, 29, 52, 67, 94
category a, 35
cell, 9
Census, 93, 96, 114
child rearing, 113
children, 43, 104, 111, 122
city, 51
civil rights, 94
clients, 71, 75
cognitive impairment, 94
cohort, viii, 5, 17, 19, 20, 43, 52, 79, 97, 98, 100, 109, 115
collateral, 109
community, 94
compatibility, 123
components, 5, 7, 8, 10, 15, 16, 20, 25, 28, 36, 53, 72
composition, 4, 98
computing, 42, 54
concentration, 106, 122
Congressional Budget Office, v, 97, 101, 103, 105, 107, 112, 114, 118, 123
construction, 8
consumer price index, 95
consumer protection, 69
consumers, 59, 70, 72, 74
consumption patterns, 53
control, 23, 52, 74, 100
correlation, 31, 76, 90, 95
correlation coefficient, 95

costs, 31, 36, 50, 61, 63, 66, 98, 101, 102, 103, 122
couples, 5, 30, 122
credit, 106
creditors, 70
CRR, 118
current account, 84, 112
current account balance, 84, 112
current balance, 88
database, 111
death, 30, 42, 48, 52, 54, 55, 56, 58, 61, 62, 75, 78, 79, 88, 96, 102, 103, 104, 122
debt, 8
decisions, 88, 106, 107, 108, 123
defined benefit pension, vii, 57, 63, 71
defined-contribution plans, 107
demographic change, 110
demographic factors, viii, 98
demographic structure, 30
demographic transition, 111
demographics, 110
Department of Health and Human Services, 93, 96
dependency ratio, 113, 114
deposits, 29
developed countries, 123
developing countries, 110
developing nations, 98
deviation, 48, 90
disclosure, 70, 71, 72
discounting, 34, 47, 48, 52, 54
dissaving, 49, 99, 100, 102, 103, 106, 112, 121
distribution, 3, 5, 18, 25, 52, 67, 75, 90, 94, 101, 105, 107, 122
divorce, 56, 58, 61
dominant strategy, 89
Dow Jones Industrial Average, 66
downsizing, 52
duration, 98
early retirement, 4
earnings, 49, 54, 64, 67, 93
economic growth, 110
economics, 11
economies of scale, 10, 12, 13, 17, 19, 30, 34
education, 96
elderly, 49, 59, 102, 103, 104, 106, 109, 113, 121
elderly population, 104
employees, 68, 96
equities, 70
equity, 28, 29, 52, 57, 62, 66, 69, 70, 71, 73, 107, 109
equity market, 57, 62, 66, 70
estimating, 19, 52, 90
estimation process, 90
European Union, 112
evolution, vii, 1, 8, 17, 18
exercise, 52
expenditures, 32, 38, 59, 102, 106, 122, 123
expertise, 70, 88
exposure, 108
extraction, 52
family, 17, 73, 100, 122
family history, 73
family members, 100
Federal Reserve Board, 1, 40, 51
fertility, 113
fertility rate, 113
finance, viii, 4, 25, 37, 38, 48, 57, 97, 98, 99, 100, 108, 110, 112, 122
financial markets, 99, 108, 116, 123
financial shocks, 58
financing, 38
flexibility, 73
fluctuations, 66, 107
focusing, 2, 4
food, 45
fraud, 70
frequency distribution, 18
funding, 63
funds, 7, 29, 57, 60, 64, 65, 67, 72, 73, 75, 89, 96, 105, 106, 107, 122
gender, 49, 64, 94
generation, vii, viii, 57, 97, 108, 123
goods and services, 60, 94

government, iv, 7, 8, 30, 37, 60, 69, 70, 123
government securities, 60
graph, 19
gross domestic product, 112
groups, 3, 4, 17, 18, 25, 28, 35, 36, 37, 50, 54, 98, 100, 103, 108, 113
growth, 23, 47, 52, 60, 62, 66, 113, 115, 123
growth factor, 23, 52
growth rate, 47
guidance, 88
guidelines, 69
health, 4, 6, 49, 50, 60, 61, 71, 73, 101, 102, 103, 122
health care, 60, 61, 101
health care costs, 61
health insurance, 102
health status, 50
heterogeneity, 35, 53
high school, 6
high school degree, 6
home ownership, 109
home value, 8
House, 96
household composition, 3, 33
household income, 3, 52
housing, viii, 3, 8, 15, 20, 28, 29, 52, 53, 98, 106, 109, 122
husband, 14, 30
hypothesis, 46
images, 118
IMF, 117
immigrants, 98, 109, 113
immigration, 110, 112, 113, 114, 123
incentives, 102
incidence, 50
inclusion, 48
income distribution, 8, 18, 23, 25, 37, 49, 102, 113
income tax, 67, 68, 69, 76
indication, 108
indicators, 23, 52
indices, 116
industry, 72
inertia, 123
inferences, 100
inflation, viii, 14, 43, 45, 52, 53, 56, 57, 58, 59, 60, 62, 65, 66, 74, 76, 79, 82, 88, 90, 95, 96, 98
injury, iv
instruments, 105, 122
insurance, 38, 54, 56, 57, 62, 63, 69, 70, 71, 72, 73, 74, 76, 83, 122
intentions, 104
interactions, 110
interest rates, 11, 60, 65
Internal Revenue Service, 67
International Monetary Fund, 117
interval, 78
intuition, 10, 54
investment, 56, 58, 59, 60, 62, 63, 64, 65, 66, 67, 69, 72, 74, 75, 77, 78, 80, 81, 84, 88, 90, 95, 96, 109, 123
investment rate, 90
investors, 70, 98, 109
jurisdiction, 69
labor, 114, 115, 123
labor force, 114, 115, 123
language, 69
laws, 69, 70, 71
leisure, 50
lens, 15
life cycle, vii, 1, 2, 3, 4, 11, 12, 13, 14, 15, 28, 29, 30, 31, 34, 35, 38, 46, 53, 101, 102, 109, 115, 122, 123
life cycle hypothesis, 11, 12
life expectancy, vii, 1, 2, 3, 11, 16, 20, 28, 46, 52, 53, 56, 57, 58, 63, 64, 67, 68, 71, 74, 75, 84, 85, 88, 94, 95, 96, 101
life span, 79, 95, 101, 102, 122
lifespan, 14
lifetime, 3, 12, 29, 52, 64, 66, 68, 72, 79, 102, 106, 122
likelihood, 59, 75, 77, 78, 79, 80, 84, 90, 122
line, 4, 20, 38, 53, 70
liquid assets, 7, 122
liquidate, 100

loans, 109
longevity, vii, 1, 4, 11, 33, 34, 38, 43, 46, 47, 53, 54, 56, 58, 62, 63, 64, 71, 73, 74, 76, 83
longitudinal study, 122
long-term care insurance, 61, 69, 73
low risk, 88
magnetic, iv
major purchases, 108
males, 49
management, 72
marital status, 9, 17, 18, 19, 25, 33, 37, 52
market, viii, 29, 53, 56, 58, 60, 62, 63, 65, 66, 70, 71, 76, 90, 94, 97, 105, 106, 107, 108, 115, 116, 122
marketing, 69, 70
markets, viii, 54, 62, 66, 97, 102, 116, 122
Markov chain, 32
married couples, 6, 8, 31, 33, 34, 35
measurement, 2
measures, 2, 5, 17, 19, 28, 43, 53, 89, 101
median, vii, 1, 3, 4, 7, 8, 15, 16, 17, 18, 20, 23, 25, 28, 29, 30, 34, 35, 37, 49, 52, 53, 61, 71, 93, 94, 100, 101, 102, 122
Medicaid, 61, 94
medical care, 6, 32, 53, 56, 58, 60, 94, 104
Medicare, 41, 50, 60, 61, 94, 102, 122
men, 30, 59, 61, 64, 79, 80, 84, 87, 95
model, vii, 1, 3, 4, 10, 11, 13, 15, 29, 30, 31, 32, 33, 34, 35, 36, 38, 45, 46, 48, 49, 51, 53, 54, 69, 75, 76, 79, 90, 95, 96, 102, 112, 122, 123
model specification, 14, 29, 33, 34, 35, 46
modeling, 29
models, vii, 1, 4, 14, 29, 38, 46, 53
money, vii, 29, 55, 64, 65, 67, 70, 71, 74, 75, 76, 77, 78, 80
Monte Carlo method, 90
mortality, 2, 30, 43, 49, 50, 54, 72, 78, 79, 80
mortality risk, 2
motives, 2, 4, 14, 15, 53, 54, 103, 104, 123
nation, 98, 122
negativity, 29, 32
nursing, 61, 94
nursing home, 61, 94
observations, 6, 7, 122
observed behavior, 4
old age, 2, 31, 32, 34, 36, 54, 59, 99, 100, 101, 102, 103, 109, 122
older people, 99, 103, 109, 122
optimization, 12, 53
order, 5, 46, 94, 98, 100, 104
oversight, 69
parameter, 30, 31, 32
parameters, 10, 30, 53
parents, 104, 122
Pension Benefit Guaranty Corporation, 94
pension plans, 43, 63, 64, 107, 109, 121
pensions, vii, viii, 5, 8, 43, 52, 53, 55, 57, 59, 63
planning, 53, 74, 79, 84, 88, 122
poor, 6, 50, 61, 100, 106
population, 5, 34, 54, 58, 71, 73, 98, 99, 101, 110, 111, 112, 113, 122, 123
portfolio, 5, 60, 72, 76, 77, 78, 79, 80, 81, 85, 86, 87, 88, 89, 95, 108, 109, 123
portfolios, 59, 65, 76, 77, 79, 80, 81, 95, 98, 100, 109
precautionary motives, 29, 34, 104
prediction, 99, 116
preference, 30, 34
premiums, 60, 64, 68, 69, 70, 73, 102, 122
present value, 5, 8, 20, 30, 42, 43, 44, 52, 54
price index, 53
prices, viii, 28, 53, 59, 60, 70, 73, 98, 99, 106, 115, 116, 123
primary data, 5

private sector, 59, 64
probability, 12, 30, 42, 44, 52, 54, 56, 58, 75, 76, 77, 78, 79, 80, 88, 90, 91, 95, 96
probability distribution, 90
product design, 72
production, 4, 30, 115
productivity, 52
productivity growth, 52
program, 60, 61, 90, 96
property, iv
purchasing power, 56, 57, 59, 66
range, 3, 20, 23, 29, 65, 76, 79, 85, 86, 87, 88, 94
rate of return, 56, 60, 64, 65, 66, 75, 76, 90, 95, 96, 123
rationality, 52
real assets, 115, 122
real income, 99
real terms, 8, 95
real wage, 115
reason, 9, 63, 71, 100
reflection, 46
region, 111
regression, 19, 23, 25, 28, 29, 52
regulation, 65, 69, 70, 71
regulations, 69, 71, 74
relationship, 32
relief, 36, 70
reserves, 83
resources, vii, 1, 2, 3, 4, 5, 8, 9, 10, 15, 18, 20, 31, 32, 36, 38, 48, 50, 113
retention, 102
retirement age, 54
retirement pension, 84
returns, 34, 60, 63, 75, 76, 84, 90
risk aversion, 31, 33, 37, 53
safety, 70, 102
sales, 52, 58, 64, 65, 66, 69, 70, 71, 72, 73, 100, 108, 111, 122
sampling, 52
savings, 2, 4, 13, 29, 36, 56, 57, 58, 59, 62, 64, 74, 75, 76, 77, 83, 89, 93, 104, 108, 114, 115, 123
savings account, 57, 64
scale economies, 17, 19
search, 29
securities, 60, 70, 71, 76
security, vii, 55
selecting, 5
Senate, 95
sensitivity, 122
services, iv
severity, 50
sex, 34, 42
shape, 25, 29, 31
shares, 7, 34, 109
shock, 4, 31, 32, 46, 54, 61
simulation, 46, 50, 75, 90, 95, 96
software, 90, 95
spectrum, 113
SSI, 45
standard deviation, 90
standard of living, 2, 59
standards, 4
state laws, 69, 70
statutes, 94
stock, viii, 7, 10, 48, 53, 60, 66, 69, 86, 90, 97, 99, 106, 107, 108, 109, 110, 115, 116, 117, 122, 123
stock markets, 106
stock price, 53
stock value, 60
strategies, 56, 58, 89
strength, viii, 32, 97, 104
subsidy, 61
success rate, 80
supply, 115, 123
Supreme Court, 94
survival, 5, 12, 14, 33, 34, 37, 42, 45, 46, 47, 48, 49, 54, 79
survival rate, 34, 49
survivors, 42, 44, 54
tax deduction, viii, 55
tax rates, 67, 94
taxation, 67, 69
tenure, 52
thinking, 2, 70, 98
time series, 116
timing, 63

trade, 84, 89
trade-off, 84, 89
trading, 109
trajectory, 2, 3, 9, 25, 38
transaction costs, 109, 122
transfer payments, 2, 5
transition, 29, 30, 113
transitions, 45
transparency, 53, 71
uncertainty, 2, 33, 37, 38, 46, 56, 98, 102
United Nations, 111
variability, 84, 90, 96
variables, 5, 79, 90, 95
variance, 31, 90
vehicles, 7, 29, 62, 64
volatile environment, 96
volatility, 57
wages, 52
wealth distribution, 106
welfare, 9, 30, 44, 51
withdrawal, 56, 58, 67, 74, 75, 76, 77, 78, 79, 80, 82, 84, 85, 86, 87, 88, 89, 95
women, 6, 30, 59, 61, 64, 79, 80, 81, 84, 87, 95
workers, 43, 53, 54, 63, 99, 115